MODERN-DAY
SERIAL
KILLERS

Don Rauf

Enslow Publishing

101 W. 23rd Street
Suite 240
New York, NY 10011
USA
enslow.com

Published in 2016 by Enslow Publishing, LLC.
101 W. 23rd Street, Suite 240, New York, NY 10011

Copyright © 2016 by Enslow Publishing, LLC.

Library of Congress Cataloging-in-Publication Data

Names: Rauf, Don, author.
Title: Modern-day serial killers / Don Rauf.
Description: New York, NY : Enslow Publishing, [2016] | Series: The
  psychology of serial killers | Includes bibliographical references and
  index.
Identifiers: LCCN 2015038956 | ISBN 9780766072985
Subjects: LCSH: Serial murderers—Juvenile literature. | Criminal
  psychology—Juvenile literature.
Classification: LCC HV6515 .R286 2016 | DDC 364.152/32--dc23
LC record available at http://lccn.loc.gov/2015038956

Printed in the United States of America

To Our Readers: We have done our best to make sure all websites in this book were active
and appropriate when we went to press. However, the author and the publisher have no
control over and assume no liability for the material available on those websites or on
any websites they may link to. Any comments or suggestions can be sent by e-mail to
custserv@enslow.com.

Contents

What is it about serial killers that fascinates us? Television shows, movies, and books that feature serial killers in main roles have become part of the popular culture.

INTRODUCTION

From all the television shows and movies today, serial killing does seem like a crime that is distinctly modern. Fictional serial killers have even become the heroes of television shows and movies. Despite the popularity of fictional serial killers, in real life, serial killing may be on the decline. James Alan Fox, a criminology professor at Northeastern University and coauthor of *Extreme Killing: Understanding Serial and Mass Murder*, kept close track of information about confirmed serial murderers starting in 1900. Before 1960, there were only about a dozen or so serial killers in the United States. After 1960, that number jumped to nineteen for the decade. Then there were 119 in the 1970s and 200 in the 1980s. The numbers then go down after that, with 141 in the 1990s and 61 in the 2000s.[1]

This isn't to say horrific murderous crimes have declined. The United States has seen a rash of frightful mass killings over the past few decades, including the murder of twenty-eight at Sandy Hook Elementary School in Connecticut, nine at a black church in South Carolina, and twelve at a movie theater in Aurora, Colorado.

In explaining the drop in the number of serial murders, Beam suggests police work may have played a role. Improved deoxyribonucleaic acid (DNA) testing has certainly made a difference in identifying more killers and arresting them before they can kill again. Perhaps people are more aware as well. For example, serial killer Edmund Kemper may have been able to abduct coeds because more people felt safe hitchhiking in the 1970s. Some say the Internet has helped as people continually post where they are and where they are going. Cell phones may be making a difference as well. Serial killer Dennis Rader would cut off a victim's connection to the outside world by snipping the phone lines. Today, people can call for help via their mobile devices.

Medicine, too, may be helping. Medical experts can better identify the warning signs of a person with homicidal tendencies, and new medications to control mental illness may have limited the numbers of individuals who turn into killing machines.

While serial killers aren't exclusively men, men dominate the field. Sex, power, manipulation, domination, and control are main motivations for serial murderers. According to Victims of Violence, a thirty-year-old Canadian charitable organization, men tend to be more actively violent in their killing, raping, torturing, beating, or strangling of their victims compared to women.[2] Male serial killers will most often target strangers, rather than family, friends, and romantic partners.

Understanding Types of Murder

Serial killing is a specific category of murder, distinct from mass murder or crimes of passion. A serial killer takes the lives of several people over a period of time. Some crime experts define serial killing as murdering more than three people over the course of a month or more. Some categorize it as the killing of two or more victims in separate events. One edition of the Federal Bureau of Investigation's (FBI's) official *Crime Classification Manual* says that for the murders to be called serial killings, there must be at least three different murders at three different locations with breaks between these events. Some killers have brought victims back to the same location, and they have been called serial killers.

A mass murderer is someone who snaps and kills a group of people. One example is Seung-Hui Cho, a student who shot and murdered thirty-two people on Virginia Tech's campus on one day in 2007. Spree killers murder in multiple locations and within a short period of time, and they may be considered a type of serial killer. In 1997, Andrew Cunanan conducted a cross-country killing spree, murdering at least five people, including the famous designer Gianni Versace. Serial killers differ from those who commit a "crime of passion." A "crime of passion" murder happens as a result of a sudden strong impulse of anger or heartbreak toward someone the killer knows. Serial killers, however, often murder strangers, although family members and friends may be their victims as well. They often take some sort of sick pleasure in killing for killing's sake. They usually work alone. There are also democidal killers who murder on behalf of their government. This may include genocide, politicide, and mass murder. Even though murderous dictators and tyrants may kill many people over time, they are generally not categorized as serial killers.

What Makes a Serial Killer?

Ernst August Ferdinand Gennat, director of Berlin's criminal police unit, may have been the first to coin the phrase "serial killer." In the

While experts don't know exactly what causes a person to become a serial killer, there are some commonalities in the childhoods of those they have studied. It turns out that many serial killers came from abusive households, suffered serious head traumas, wet the bed longer than normal, were cruel to animals, and regularly set things on fire.

1930s, he dubbed Peter Kürten as a *serienmörder* or, in English, a serial killer. Kürten was given the nickname "the Vampire of Düsseldorf" and "the Düsseldorf Monster" for killing nine women and girls. The term became a more common part of the language when FBI Special Agent Robert Ressler used it in reference to David Berkowitz (also known as "The Son of Sam"), who killed six people over a period of time in New York City from 1976 to 1977.[3]

In a paper published in 1963 in the *American Journal of Psychiatry*, titled "The Threat to Kill," psychiatrist John Macdonald first identified three characteristics that are telltale signs in childhood that a person may have homicidal tendencies later in life. The three traits are animal cruelty, setting fires, and persistent bed-wetting. As you read through the profiles in this book, you will see that many of the serial killers had these traits when they were young, but experts have cast doubt on the true predictive value of these characteristics. A child may exhibit these characteristics and not be murder-prone at all. In profiles of serial killers, however, these actions are often displayed.[4]

Jim Fallon, a neuroscientist and professor at the University of California, has been studying the brains of psychopathic killers. In a TED (Technology, Entertainment, Design) Talk that he gave in July 2009, he said that he has studied many brains and the ones belonging to murderers and serial killers all had "damage to their orbital cortex, which is right above the eyes, the orbits, and also the interior part of the temporal lobe."[5] They may have been born with the damage, or it may come later. Many of the modern serial killers profiled here suffered a traumatic brain injury early in their lives.

Another common thread seen in the profiles of serial killers is a troubled family life. The father or sometimes the mother may be absent or very abusive. Serial killers may also have problems with alcohol or drug abuse.

The psychologist Sigmund Freud studied human behavior extensively. According to Freud's theory of personality development, behavior is shaped mostly by the interactions that the child has with the world before the age of five. How an infant is treated is crucial to his or her development. If a person does not have adequate touch, love, and support as a child, he or she can develop a personality disorder. Many serial killers have suffered some sort of child abuse. Many were in difficult family situations or had absent parents. Some studies show that 16 percent of serial killers were adopted. An article from Le Moyne College in Syracuse titled "Psychology of a Serial Killer" presents these statistics about convicted serial killers:

- **42** percent suffered from physical abuse as children.
- **74** percent suffered from psychological abuse.
- **35** percent witnessed sexual abuse.
- **43** percent were sexually abused themselves.
- **29** percent were found to be accident-prone children.[6]

Psychopathic vs. Psychotic

One way that psychologists distinguish types of serial killers is by categorizing them as either psychopathic (or organized) or psychotic (or disorganized). Former FBI profiler Roy Hazelwood helped create this structure or approach to better understand serial killers, according to an article in *Business Insider*.[7]

The Crime Museum in Washington, DC, explains the two types.[8] Organized killers are often clever and fairly meticulous. They plan carefully and go through great pains to make sure they do not leave clues as to their identity. They may track potential victims for days, deciding who will be a suitable target. They are often well-equipped with tools, locations, and details on how to kill and dispose of a person. They often gain the trust of a person, faking emotions or gaining sympathy. They typically seem like very normal people. They often take great pride in how they are able to kill and get away with

Criminologists have used several different classifications in their studies of serial killers. The FBI categorizes serial killers as either organized, disorganized, or mixed. They are further classified by their motives for killing: visionary, mission-oriented, hedonistic, and power/control-oriented.

it. These killers are psychopaths—people who suffer from chronic mental disorders and exhibit abnormal or violent social behaviors. Sometimes they will take pleasure in stumping law enforcement professionals who are trying to catch them.

Disorganized serial killers do not plan at all. Their victims just happen to be in the wrong place at the wrong time. These killers seem to murder just when the moment and circumstances feel right. They usually make no effort to cover up their crimes. They are likely to leave blood, fingerprints, and the murder weapon behind.

Modern-Day Serial Killers

Their violent acts are often messy. They move around to different locations, towns, and states to avoid capture. They typically have lower intelligence quotients (IQs) than the organized killers. They may feel compelled by visions or voices they hear in their head. They usually have a form of psychosis, an extreme mental disorder in which thoughts and emotions are so impaired that they have lost a grasp on reality. They have an inability to maintain relationships, and they may be abusing drugs or alcohol.

Sometimes the criminals are "mixed offenders" who cannot be easily classified as either organized or disorganized.

The profiles of serial killers in this resource give a glimpse into the motivations behind a murderer's actions, and the incidents and circumstances that may have shaped their lives and horrific crimes. Note that while the killers here are separated into different categories, they often have traits that make them fit into several categories.

Method of disposal	May dismember body after killing; disposes of remains	Leaves body behind after killing; usually does not dismember
State of crime scene	Controlled; little physical evidence left behind	Chaotic; leaves physical evidence behind
Reason for returning to scene of crime	To see the police working; interest in police work	To relive the murder

Source: O'Connor, Tom. "Serial Killer Typology."

http://www.ravenndragon.net/montgomery/csi/oconnortypology1.pdf

Chapter 1

PSYCHOTIC KILLERS

Some serial killers are categorized as psychotic or disorganized. Many in this category are visionary serial killers, who are motivated to take action because they have hallucinations that command them to kill.[1] These killers take lives in an almost random manner. They don't plan things out, and they usually kill people who happen to present the opportunity to murder.

Richard Chase

aka "The Vampire Killer" or "The Vampire of Sacramento"

Born: May 23, 1950

Location: Sacramento, California

Profession: No known jobs

Diagnosis: Paranoid schizophrenia

Date of capture: January 1978

Date of death: December 26, 1980 (in prison)

"Everyone has a soap dish. If you lift the soap and find that underneath it is dry, you're all right. If it's gooey, you have the poisoning, which turns your blood to powder. The powder then depletes your energy and eats away at your body." These were the words of Richard Chase, who was diagnosed as schizophrenic, a condition characterized by withdrawal from reality, illogical patterns of thinking, delusions, hallucinations, and psychotic behavior.

Chase had a delusion that Nazis planted poison in his soap dish and this poison would turn his blood to powder. He believed he had to kill and drink blood to reverse the effects of this poison and keep himself alive. Chase's psychological troubles began at an early age. He was raised by a mentally ill mother and an alcoholic father. His father was very strict and argumentative. At age eight, Chase was still wetting his bed, and in the next two years, he started setting fires

Richard Chase's mental problems, including schizophrenia, drove him to murder. Plagued with delusions and visions, he believed that he was being poisoned by Nazis through his soap dish. Chase killed and feasted on animals before turning his murderous acts on humans.

and drinking the blood of animals that he killed. Even at this age, he had a notion that he had to drink blood to refresh his blood, which was being poisoned.

In addition, he had many other odd habits, such as holding an orange with the belief that he could absorb the vitamin C through his skin. There were constant fights in his family, and his mother sought mental help when Chase was twelve years old. Soon after, the family had a serious financial hardship and lost their home. Richard was a poor student and just barely graduated high school.

After turning eighteen, he moved out on his own and turned to drugs. He couldn't get or keep a job, so his father paid for his apartment. Chase's delusions grew around a type of hypochondria. He'd often go to the hospital emergency room seeking help for impossible ailments—he believed his stomach was in backwards, his pulmonary artery was missing, and his heart had stopped. Finally, after a psychiatric evaluation, he was declared to be a paranoid schizophrenic.

Chase thought the cure for his problems was to kill small animals and eat their raw insides. He was hospitalized again after injecting himself with rabbit blood. In 1976, he was committed to a mental institution called Beverly Manor. One day an orderly found two dead birds on Chase's windowsill. Their necks were broken, and Chase had blood around his mouth.

After a short confinement, doctors decided that Chase was not a danger to others and released him under the care of his parents. His mother decided that he no longer needed his antischizophrenia medication, and that led to increasing problems. Chase caught more cats, dogs, and rabbits—killing them and drinking their blood. He showed a fascination with the notorious Hillside Strangler

Chase was obsessed with the Hillside Strangler, a serial killer on the loose in Los Angeles around the time Chase committed his acts of murder. The Hillside Strangler turned out to be two men, Angelo Buono and his cousin Kenneth Bianchi, pictured above.

and collected articles about him. He bought a car and drove into Nevada, where he cut the liver from a live cow and sat naked in his car covered in cow blood.

In early December of 1977, Chase bought a .22 automatic pistol for $70. At the end of the month, he fired shots out of his car window and killed a random man who was helping his wife bring in the groceries. In January of 1978, he crept into a pregnant woman's home. He shot her dead, mutilated her, and performed depraved sex acts on her corpse. At the end of the month, he committed his last, random act of horrific violence. He entered the home of Evelyn Miroth and killed her, her six-year-old son, her male friend, and her twenty-two-month-old nephew, whom she was babysitting. He engaged in necrophilia and cannibalism. Hand and shoe prints left at the scene led police to Chase. He was sentenced to death but killed himself in prison with an overdose of his antidepressants.[2,3,4]

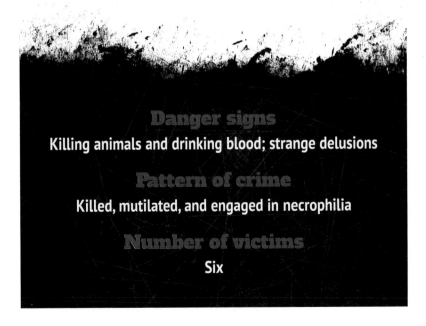

Danger signs

Killing animals and drinking blood; strange delusions

Pattern of crime

Killed, mutilated, and engaged in necrophilia

Number of victims

Six

Richard Ramirez
aka "The Night Stalker"

Born: February 29, 1960

Profession: Car mechanic, Holiday Inn employee, miscellaneous

Motive: Gain

Date of capture: August 25, 1985

Date of death: June 7, 2013 (in prison)

Born into a strict Catholic home in El Paso, Texas, Richard Ramirez had a life that looked like trouble right from the start. His mother had been exposed to many toxic chemicals at a boot factory: She quit her job while pregnant with Richard because the fumes were making her nauseous and light-headed. His three older brothers were plagued with either learning disabilities or poor health. Ramirez's mother was hopeful that Richard would have better luck. Ramirez's father worked hard as a laborer on the Santa Fe railroad. He was quick to anger, often turning physically abusive.

His parents thought of Ramirez as a "good boy." Unfortunately, he suffered a head injury at age two when a dresser fell on top of him as he tried to climb it. Then at age five, a swing hit him in the head. He experienced several epileptic seizures after this accident. His uncle Mike Ramirez gave fuel to perverse fantasies when he told the teenage Richard about his exploits as a Green Beret in Vietnam.

BK 7867407 121284

LOS ANGELES POLICE — JAIL - F

Like so many serial killers, Richard Ramirez suffered several blows to the head during his childhood. He earned the title "Night Stalker" for his habit of invading homes at night and robbing, raping, murdering, and mutilating the sleeping inhabitants. The disturbed killer never showed remorse for any of his brutal acts.

Uncle Mike showed Richard photos of Vietnamese women he had raped, mutilated, and murdered. Some of the photos showed the severed heads of his victims. Uncle Mike and Richard would also get high on marijuana and talk about Satan worship. Richard was in the room when Uncle Mike had a heated argument with his wife and shot her in the face, killing her. His uncle was found not guilty by reason of insanity.

While in high school at the age of fifteen, Richard briefly held a job at a Holiday Inn. He was attracted to the pretty women who stayed there. One day his urges got the better of him, and he tried to rape a guest in her room. Her husband appeared and stopped it. Richard's parents could not believe that their baby would do such a thing, and Richard told them he was seduced. He got off with leniency because of his young age.

At age twenty, he left El Paso to make Los Angeles his new home. While he reportedly worked briefly as an auto mechanic, Ramirez supported himself in Los Angeles by robbing homes. He would sell the stolen goods to get drug money. He loved heavy metal music, especially the band AC/DC and their song "Night Prowler." He started taking harder drugs such as phenylcyclohexyl piperidine (PCP) or "angel dust." He was more and more interested in Satanism. He eventually claimed to be the right-hand man of Satan. Ramirez was developing violent fantasies, and he wanted to see if he could make them a reality.

In May 1984, he began murdering people. His first victim was Mei Leung, a nine-year-old who was found in the basement of her San Francisco apartment. (This murder was a cold case for years and wouldn't be tied to Ramirez until 2004, when DNA testing found him to be the perpetrator.) Back in Los Angeles in June, Ramirez continued to leave a trail of blood. On June 28, 1984, he snuck through an open window into the home of seventy-nine-year-old Jennie Varlow. He sexually assaulted her and stabbed her in the neck repeatedly and with such force that he almost decapitated her.

He would wait about nine months before striking again on March 17, 1985. Ramirez approached twenty-year-old Angela Barrios as she was parking her car in the garage of her condo. As he pointed a gun toward her face, she pleaded with Ramirez not to kill her. She held her hands in front of her face in response. When Ramirez pulled the trigger, she dropped to the ground and he stepped over her and headed into her condo. Barrios, however, was still alive. Through some miracle, the bullet hit her keys and had ricocheted away from her. She got up and ran. Her roommate was not so lucky. Ramirez entered the condo and shot her through the forehead.

Apparently, the murder didn't satisfy Ramirez and later that night he assaulted and killed another woman. Three days later he sexually abused an eight-year-old girl. On March 27, 1985, he broke into the home of Vincent and Maxine Zazarra. He killed Vincent instantly with a gunshot. He stripped Maxine and horribly mutilated her, gouging her eyes out. He went on to assault more than twenty-five people in all, murdering more than a dozen.

Ramirez often left satanic signs at the murder scenes. The media dubbed him "The Night Stalker." His last attack on August 24, 1985, led to his capture. Again, he attacked a couple, shooting the man in the head and raping the wife. He forced the woman to say "I love Satan" repeatedly. The woman was left to live, and she got a glimpse of Ramirez's car as he sped off. A local teen happened to jot down part of the license plate number. These details led police

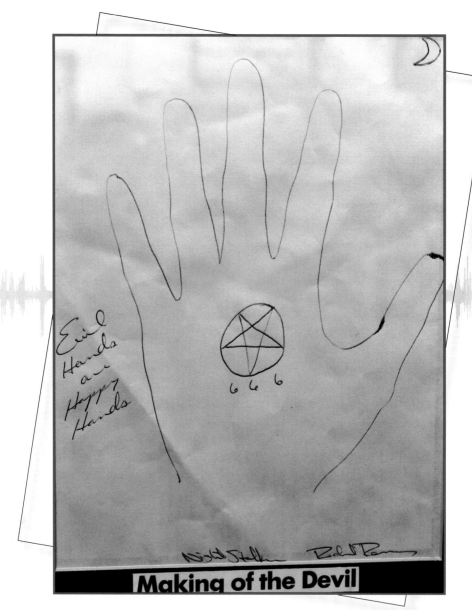

Making of the Devil

Ramirez was proud of his horrendous deeds and reveled in the celebrity of being the Night Stalker. From prison he capitalized on people's fascination with him, sending out memorabilia such as this outline of his hand bearing a satanic reference, along with his autograph.

to Ramirez's stolen car, where they found a fingerprint. Authorities were able to match the fingerprint to Ramirez.

The next day his photo was on the front page of every newspaper in Los Angeles. Ramirez only realized this when he walked into a drugstore and saw everyone staring at him. He saw his photo in the paper and ran. People yelled after him. A crowd of locals caught him, and the police arrived to arrest him.

Ramirez was brought to trial, and on September 20, 1989, the jury returned a unanimous guilty verdict on forty-three charges, including thirteen counts of murder, five counts of attempted murder, eleven sexual assault charges, and fourteen burglary charges. When he received his death sentence, he said, "Big deal! Death always went with the territory. See you in Disneyland!" He was awaiting execution on death row when he died of liver failure due to complications from blood cancer on June 7, 2013.[5,6,7,8]

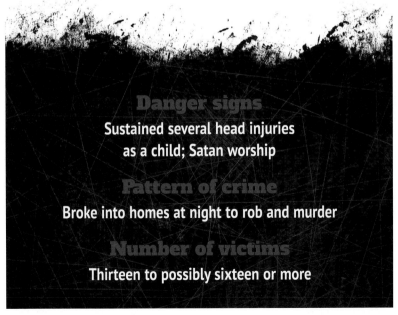

Danger signs

Sustained several head injuries
as a child; Satan worship

Pattern of crime

Broke into homes at night to rob and murder

Number of victims

Thirteen to possibly sixteen or more

David Berkowitz

*aka "The Son of Sam" or
"The .44 Caliber Killer"*

Born: June 1, 1953

Profession: Security guard, US postal worker

Diagnosis: Paranoid schizophrenic;
exhibited traits of organized
and disorganized killer

Date of capture: August 10, 1977

Date of death: Serving six life sentences

On April 16, 1977, Valentina Suriani, age eighteen, and twenty-year-old Alexander Esau were sitting in a car at 3 AM in the Bronx after having seen a late-night movie. Suddenly, four gunshots rang out, and the young couple was dead. When police arrived at the scene, they found a note addressed to Captain Joe Borelli. Part of it read: "I am a monster. I am the 'Son of Sam.' I am a little brat. . . . Sam loves to drink blood. 'Go out and kill,' commands father Sam."

The note had been left by David Berkowitz, a serial killer who terrorized New York City during the summer of 1977. To add to the panic of having a serial killer on the loose, the city suffered through heat waves and a major blackout on July 13. By this point, Berkowitz had killed five random and innocent people, and he had wounded several others. He targeted young single women and couples. He would sneak up on them and blast away with his .44 caliber Bulldog

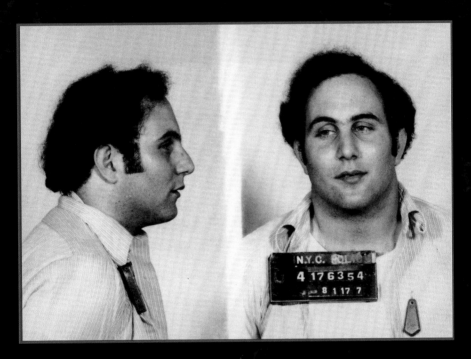

David Berkowitz believed that a neighbor's dog was ordering him to kill. The disturbed Berkowitz liked to prey on young couples, particularly on women with long dark hair.

snubnose revolver. One woman he simply shot in the head as she walked down the street.

His notes taunted police who had yet to identify that the killer was Berkowitz. He also sent a note to one of his favorite columnists, Jimmy Breslin at the *New York Daily News*. A portion of his letter read: "I am still here. Like a spirit roaming the night. Thirsty, hungry, seldom stopping to rest; anxious to please Sam. I love my work. Now, the void has been filled." The city was in a panic, and Berkowitz's letters were fueling the public imagination about a crazed killer on the loose.

The police finally caught a break on July 31, 1977; unfortunately, one more young person would lose her life before Berkowitz was caught. On this night, he shot Bobby Violante and Stacy Moskowitz, who were on a first date. Berkowitz seemed to be targeting brunettes—Moskowitz was blond, so the couple felt relatively safe. Berkowitz's gunfire killed Moskowitz and left Violante blind in one eye and partially sightless in the other. A witness spotted the gunman driving off in a car with a parking ticket on the windshield. By reviewing the tickets given out that day, police were able to identify the suspect as twenty-four-year-old David Berkowitz, a letter sorter for the US post office.

After police arrested him on August 10, Berkowitz told them that his neighbor's dog had told him to kill. In the months to come, mental health experts determined that Berkowitz had mental, emotional, and behavioral problems that could be traced back to his childhood. Berkowitz was an adopted child. At age seven, he was in a car accident and suffered head injuries. He became a loner and was teased for his chubbiness. He had bad bouts of depression and was suicidal. At ages twelve and thirteen, he set fires and tortured

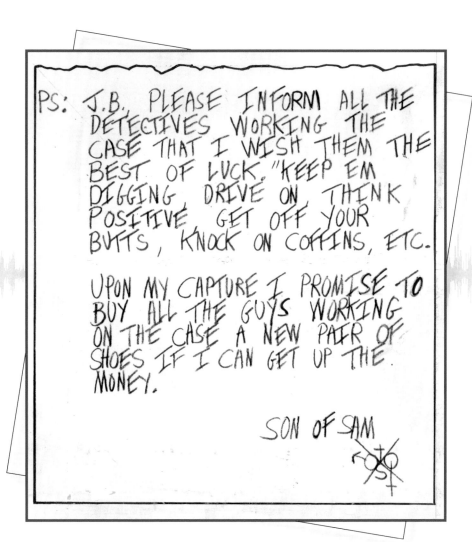

PS: J.B., PLEASE INFORM ALL THE DETECTIVES WORKING THE CASE THAT I WISH THEM THE BEST OF LUCK. "KEEP EM DIGGING, DRIVE ON, THINK POSITIVE, GET OFF YOUR BUTTS, KNOCK ON COFFINS, ETC.

UPON MY CAPTURE I PROMISE TO BUY ALL THE GUYS WORKING ON THE CASE A NEW PAIR OF SHOES IF I CAN GET UP THE MONEY.

SON OF SAM

Dubbed "The Son of Sam" by the press, Berkowitz began to enjoy the celebrity status he gained from terrorizing New York City. He boldly sent letters to the police and to the press, including this one, sent to reporter Jimmy Breslin at the *New York Daily News*.

New York Police Department (NYPD) officers and detectives investigate the Cadillac where Sal Lupo and Judy Placido were shot by David Berkowitz in Bayside, Queens, on June 26, 1977. Both survived, but neither could identify their attacker.

and killed animals—a pet parakeet and bugs. He became more despondent when his adoptive mother died at fourteen, and his academic performance at school sank. At age twenty-one, he shot a German shepherd. He had difficulties with the opposite sex. In 1975, he wrote his father a letter that might have been a warning of things to come: "The girls call me ugly and they bother me the most. The guys just laugh. Things will soon change for the better." When he had sex for the first time, it was with a prostitute while serving in the army, and he contracted a venereal disease.

A combination of social insecurities, resentment toward women, and mental issues appear to have driven him to kill. He was convinced that Satan would set him free of his emotional pain and loneliness through the act of murder. Berkowitz said, "The demons never stopped. I couldn't sleep. I had no strength to fight. I could barely drive. Coming home from work one night, I almost killed myself in the car. I needed to sleep...The demons wouldn't give me any peace." Berkowitz is currently serving a 365-year sentence and has become a born-again Christian, apologizing for his crimes and the sorrow he created. He has said he is no longer Son of Sam but Son of Hope.[9,10,11,12]

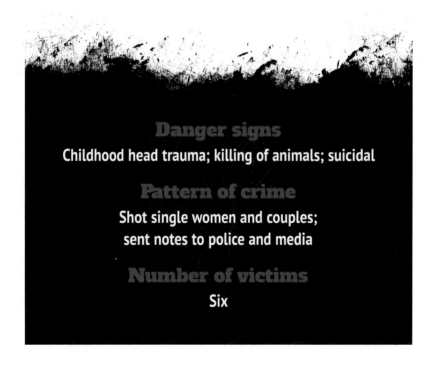

Danger signs

Childhood head trauma; killing of animals; suicidal

Pattern of crime

**Shot single women and couples;
sent notes to police and media**

Number of victims

Six

Chapter 2

PROSTITUTE SERIAL KILLERS

Many serial-killing men murder because they find a sexual thrill in killing. Some find a sadistic joy in the killing itself. Many men who experience this have targeted prostitutes. Prostitutes are considered easy prey because they are accessible and because their absence often goes unnoticed. In addition, it has been suggested that police do not focus efforts on solving prostitutes' murders as strongly as they do those of citizens who lead low-risk lives.

Gary Ridgway
aka "The Green River Killer"

Born: **February 18, 1949**

Profession: **Painter at a truck factory**

Motive: **Lust, thrill**

Date of capture: **November 30, 2001**

Date of death: **Serving forty-eight consecutive life terms**

After Gary Ridgway was arrested in 2001, the mild-mannered truck painter told detectives that he was good at just one thing: killing prostitutes. Ridgway is remarkable in that he was able to kill so many people for so long without getting caught.

Ridgway wet his bed until he was a teenager and has admitted to feeling humiliated by this and by his mother. He confessed to lusting after his mother and also wanting to stab her. Ridgway did very poorly in school and has a low IQ. At age sixteen, Ridgway said he stabbed a young boy, who survived. Upon graduating high school, he served in the military in Vietnam, where he had unprotected sex with prostitutes. In Vietnam, he contracted a venereal disease, which always angered him. When he returned home from the war, he landed a job in Renton, Washington, near Seattle, painting trucks. He kept the job for thirty years, until his eventual arrest.

Ridgway married three times. He had several girlfriends and a son. His wives said he had an unusually strong desire for sex.

Gary Ridgway was convicted of murdering forty-nine women, mostly prostitutes and runaways, over a twenty-year span. The killer targeted these victims because he had both an unquenchable thirst for sex and great shame over it.

His second wife said that he was fanatical about the Bible and religion. He wanted her to follow the strict teachings of his church pastor.

In the early 1980s, he began picking up prostitutes and runaways along Route 99 near Seattle and killing them. To win their trust, he would sometimes show them a photo of his son. He would have sex with them in his truck, at home, or in a secluded area, then strangle them from behind using a wire ligature. Ridgway dumped their bodies in wooded areas near the Green River. He said he picked prostitutes because they were easy prey and he thought they would never be reported as missing. The fact that he had to pay for sex would fuel his murderous rage.

By 1984, the local authorities had formed an official Green River task force to investigate the murders. They even consulted with serial killer Ted Bundy on the case, but his information proved to be of little use. Ridgway was arrested a couple of times on charges relating to prostitution, and he became a suspect in the case. Police kept hair and saliva samples from him so they would have a record of his DNA.

In 2001, detectives were able to use newly developed DNA technology that showed a match between Ridgway and the victims. In December 2001, he was arrested on four counts of murder, and he would eventually confess to forty-eight. An additional conviction was added as part of his plea bargain, bringing the total number of murders to forty-nine, although Ridgway had made the claim of possibly killing up to eighty women. On December 18, 2003, Ridgway was sentenced to forty-eight life sentences with no possibility of parole.[1,2]

Members of the Green River task force search a hillside near Kent, Washington, in hopes of finding the remains of one of Gary Ridgway's victims.

Danger signs

Wetting the bed; rage against women

Pattern of crime

Strangled prostitutes and runaways

Number of victims

Forty-nine but possibly as many as seventy or eighty

Lonnie Franklin Jr.
aka *"The Grim Sleeper"*

Born: **August 30, 1952**

Profession: **Garbage man**

Motive: **Lust**

Date of capture: **July 7, 2010**

Date of death: **Franklin is alive and awaiting trial**

South Los Angeles was a hard place to live in the 1980 and 1990s—neighborhoods were wracked with poverty, gang violence was common, and many young people were getting addicted to crack. Starting in 1985, a number of young, mostly African-American women in the area were being murdered. Strangled or shot, their corpses were found in dumpsters or alleys. Someone almost seemed to be hunting female prostitutes and drug addicts.

Police named their unknown murderer "The Southside Slayer." They also called the killings "the strawberry murders." (Locals referred to prostitutes who performed sex acts in exchange for small rocks of crack as "strawberries.") After eight similar murders occurred between 1985 and 1988, slayings matching the killer's work appeared to have stopped. But then three similar murders occurred in 2002, 2003, and 2007, and the killer was renamed "The Grim Sleeper" because he seemed to have taken a break.

By all accounts, Lonnie Franklin appeared to be an innocuous member of the community. Underneath his easygoing, everyman persona, however, lay a cold-blooded killer who used and disposed of women like the trash he collected.

Locals were angry that the police did not show more concern over the murders. Documentary filmmaker Nick Broomfield said that the Los Angeles Police Department (LAPD) police would designate the bodies of prostitutes as "N.H.I.," meaning "no human involved." It was a cold and telling way that showed how little regard there was for prostitutes. People believed that the case received less attention also because the victims were black and lived in poor neighborhoods.

In 2010, detectives were able to take DNA evidence from a crime scene and trace the killings to fifty-seven-year-old Lonnie Franklin, a trash collector and garage attendant for the LAPD. The police tested his DNA from saliva left on the remains of pizza slices that Franklin ate. The DNA proved to be a match to DNA found on the dead women.

Like other serial murderers who have gone undetected for years, Franklin appeared to be an ordinary person. The easygoing, stocky garbage man read romance novels and helped neighbors string Christmas lights and repair their cars. People recognized him driving around town in his orange Pinto. He lived in a comfortable home with his wife of thirty-two years. If anything raised suspicions, it was Franklin's three cell phones—he had one for work, one for family calls, and one most likely to contact prostitutes.

When police came to search his home, they found clues that Franklin might have a darker side. In his home were hidden handguns, unexplained pieces of jewelry, and 500 photographs, many containing graphic sexual images. Police said that the women in the photos often looked asleep, unconscious, or dead, and some of the victims were identified in these photographs. There were also X-rated videos that Franklin had filmed of women. Investigators

On July 7, 2010, LAPD detectives removed evidence and other items from Lonnie Franklin's home in South Los Angeles. Police found that Franklin's home, where he lived with his wife and son, was centrally located to the chain of alleys and dumpsters where Franklin would dispose of the bodies of his victims.

believed that many of the watches, rings, necklaces, and earrings found were keepsakes from his victims. Analysts on the case believe that Franklin viewed prostitutes like the trash he collected. They were meant to be used and thrown away.

When Franklin was identified as the killer, survivors of his attacks came forward, some recalling his orange Pinto. One remembered him as looking tidy and kind of geeky. When he attacked her, she blacked out, but she remembered him taking photos of her with a Polaroid camera. Somehow, she lived through his assault. While DNA evidence may indicate his guilt, thanks to lengthy pretrial delays, Franklin has yet to be tried as of this writing.[3,4,5]

Danger signs

None

Pattern of crime

Strangled or shot prostitutes

Number of victims

Eleven

Robert Hansen
aka "The Butcher Baker"

Born: **February 15, 1939**
Location: **Anchorage, Alaska**
Profession: **Baker**
Motive: **Resentment and hatred toward women that might have been based on rejections during high school**
Date of capture: **June 1983**
Date of death: **August 21, 2014 (in prison)**

One of the women whom Robert Hansen tried to kill later described him as looking like "the perfect dork." He was small with big glasses and scarred by acne. As a teen, the skinny Hansen stammered. He described his face at the time as "one big pimple." He had no social life and no real time to develop one because his father had him working most of his free time at the family bakery in Pocahontas, Iowa. Because girls showed no interest in him, he grew up hating them. Almost as if it were taken from a movie plot, Hansen vowed to get revenge on women and the world.

After he left school, he continued to work for his father and enlisted in the US Army Reserve. He later worked as a drill instructor at a police academy. It seemed the nerdy Hansen was trying to

Robert Hansen proudly poses with the horns of a trophy Dall sheep he had bagged. The expert marksman used his resources as an outdoorsman to rape, hunt down, and murder many of the women he picked up from Anchorage strip clubs.

toughen himself up. At age twenty-one, Hansen married a young woman, but his simmering resentment about his high school life appeared to get the better of him. He turned to arson and burned down a school bus garage. Discovering this abnormal behavior, his wife divorced him. Hansen served twenty months of a three-year sentence.

Once free, Hansen remarried. He and his new wife took off to Anchorage, Alaska, to start a new life. Anchorage suited Hansen well. The couple opened a bakery and had two children. His experience in the Reserves translated well to the outdoorsman life. He took up hunting and became an expert marksman. Business was good, and he bought his own small plane. He used bow and arrow and a rifle to hunt high mountain sheep, wolves, and bears.

At age thirty-three, however, Hansen's darker impulses began taking over. He was arrested for the abduction and attempted rape of a housewife and the rape of a prostitute. He served six months in prison. Surprisingly, his wife stuck with him through this. He came up with a new plan to feed his sexual desires and not get caught. In the seedy part of Anchorage, there were many strip clubs, and Hansen found that for $300 he could get women to come with him anywhere he liked. Because he seemed nerdy and harmless, women trusted him. He would fly them into the wilderness along the Knik River and rape his victims. If they submitted to all his perverse whims, he would let them live but threaten to turn them into the police for their prostitution. If a prostitute did not please him or angered him, he would set her free from his cabin and then hunt her down.

When he was caught he described how one victim cut her feet as she ran. She hid under a bush, but when Hansen called her name, she darted into a clearing where Hansen picked her off using his .223 caliber Ruger Mini-14 rifle. Sometimes he would use his hunting knife. Hansen said, "It was like going after a trophy Dall sheep or a grizzly bear."

In 1977, in the midst of his murdering, Hansen was imprisoned a short time for shoplifting a chain saw. At this time, he was diagnosed with bipolar disorder and prescribed lithium, but it's doubtful he took his medication. Prostitutes were coming and going in Alaska, so his crimes were going unnoticed, but when bodies started to be discovered in shallow graves in the 1980s, police began to suspect a serial killer was at work.

On June 13, 1983, Hansen picked up a prostitute and brought her to his home basement in Anchorage, where he brutally assaulted her. When he was finished, he told her that they were now going to take a plane flight to his hunter's cabin in the wild. As they arrived at the plane, the prostitute made a run for it. He chased her, but another car came along and saved her in the nick of time. Barefoot and handcuffed, she was able to give police enough information so they could track down Hansen as the assailant.

When confronted, Hansen was very calm and polite. He said that his wife and children were in Europe and he had been with two friends. Hansen was so convincing that the officers began to doubt the prostitute's story. Because she would not submit to a lie detector test, no charges were filed against him.

Three months later, another woman's body was found. One Alaska State Trooper still held suspicions about Hansen. Armed with a warrant, police returned to Hansen to search his house. They found weapons used in the murders, as well as identifications from the missing women and other belongings, such as

In the flats along Alaska's Knik River, criminal investigators participated in a massive search for the remains of missing prostitutes and topless dancers from the Anchorage area. Authorities were later able to link the murders to Robert Hansen, based on his psychological profile and his ownership of an airplane.

a necklace that had been custom-made for one of the victims. Hansen finally confessed. Because he had kept detailed records of where he had buried the bodies, he could help the police find the missing women. On February 18, 1984, he was sentenced to life in prison. He died incarcerated on August 21, 2014.[6,7,8]

Danger signs

Severe hatred of women

Pattern of crime

Raped prostitutes and hunted them for sport

Number of victims

Seventeen to twenty-one

Robert Pickton

Born: **October 26, 1949**

Profession: **Pig farmer**

Motive: **Thrill**

Date of capture: **February 22, 2002**

Date of death: **Serving a life sentence, with no possibility of parole for twenty-five years**

Beginning in the early 1980s and continuing until 2002, prostitutes in Vancouver, Canada, began disappearing. Traditionally, prostitutes were not very high on the list of police concerns. Because these sex workers often left town on their own volition, it was difficult to tell if they were truly missing. Many men were considered suspects in these murders, but the police could not get a solid lead.

Finally, in 1998, task force detectives followed a lead: A man named Bill Hiscox had been working on the Pickton pig farm in nearby Port Coquitlam. The Picktons were multimillionaires who had extensive property and a slaughterhouse. From the moment he started working at the farm, Hiscox said he felt a creepy vibe. A humungous and mean 600-pound (272-kilogram) boar patrolled the grounds, chasing intruders and biting at them.

Hiscox had been reading about missing women, and he thought that Robert "Willie" Pickton might be a possible suspect. Willie was

Robert Pickton, the very wealthy owner of a successful pig farm in British Columbia, Canada, confessed to an undercover police officer that he wanted to kill one more person so he could bring his victim count to an even fifty. It is believed that Pickton fed the remains of some of his victims to his pigs. Some say that he may even have mixed some of the remains with pork that he sold to customers.

slow but not retarded. He never drank or smoked, but he frequented prostitutes. Hiscox learned that Willie and his brother David often had parties in a converted building on the farm that they called "The Piggy Palace." The brothers supposedly threw the events for charity under a nonprofit they formed called "The Piggy Palace Good Times Society," but Hiscox said the parties were drunken raves filled with prostitutes. Relatives of missing prostitutes said some women never returned from these parties. Police eventually banned the Picktons from throwing parties because they were not licensed to do so.

In 1992, Willie was charged with sexual assault. His victim told police that Pickton had attacked her in his trailer at the pig farm, but she managed to escape. The punishment: a $1,000 fine. In 1997, Pickton was arrested for attempted murder when he handcuffed a prostitute and tried to stab her. The case was dismissed because authorities said the prostitute was not a reliable witness.

Because of this history and Pickton's continued hiring of prostitutes from the "Low Track," Vancouver's equivalent of Skid Row, Hiscox told police his suspicions. Investigators searched the farm three times and found nothing. After 1999, relatives of the missing women and other women's organizations began to hold rallies demanding that the police treat the missing women more seriously and devote more time and energy to finding them.

On February 5, 2002, police received a tip that Willie Pickton possessed unregistered guns on his farm. Police raided the farm and found belongings of some of the missing women. Other confiscated items were tested for DNA, and investigators found DNA from some of the missing women.

Pickton was arrested on February 22. According to testimony, Pickton liked to handcuff a prostitute, have sex, and then strangle

Investigators from the Royal Canadian Mounted Police moved debris from Robert Pickton's pig farm on February 19, 2002. The investigators engaged in large-scale excavation efforts, finding evidence of remains and the DNA of thirty-three victims.

her with a belt or wire. A friend of Pickton's testified, saying that Pickton suggested a good way to kill a female heroin addict was to inject her with windshield-washer fluid. Pickton would take the corpses to the slaughterhouse to bleed and gut them. He would put the remains in a woodchipper and feed them to his pigs.

On March 10, 2004, it was revealed that human flesh may have been ground up and mixed with pork from the farm. Pickton appeared to get a perverse pleasure from killing. He told a police officer that he regretted that he didn't get to kill one more time because then he would have reached an even fifty murders. On December 11, 2007, Pickton was given a life sentence in prison with no possibility of parole for twenty-five years.[9,10,11,12]

Danger signs

Possible mental problems; regular client of prostitutes

Pattern of crime

Handcuffed and raped victims before strangling them and feeding their remains to his pigs

Number of victims

Six to forty-nine

Chapter 3

SEXUAL PREDATORS

While those who target prostitutes and other sex workers specifically are considered sexual predators, there are some serial killers who specifically see their victims as sexual prey. John Wayne Gacy focused on teenage boys. Dennis Rader picked out random women and individuals to satisfy his lust. Kenneth Bianchi focused on torturing, raping, and killing women.

John Wayne Gacy
aka "The Killer Clown"

Born: **March 17, 1942**

Profession: **Restaurant manager, building contractor, children's party clown**

Motive: **Lust**

Date of capture: **December 21, 1978**

Date of death: **May 10, 1994 (executed)**

John Wayne Gacy stands out from all other serial killers because in his spare time he dressed as "Pogo the Clown" and entertained children in the local hospital. The idea of a killer clown is an iconic horror image today, and it has its roots in the depraved behavior of John Wayne Gacy. Like many other successful serial killers, Gacy is frightening because of how he seamlessly blended in with society. He attended a business college and realized his natural talent as a salesman. In 1964, he married a woman whose parents had a string of Kentucky Fried Chicken restaurants in Waterloo, Iowa. Gacy became an industrious restaurant manager in Waterloo, becoming heavily involved in community groups, including the Catholic Inter-Club Council and the Jaycees. The Jaycees, in fact, called him an outstanding vice president in 1967. He and his wife completed their family with a son and a daughter.

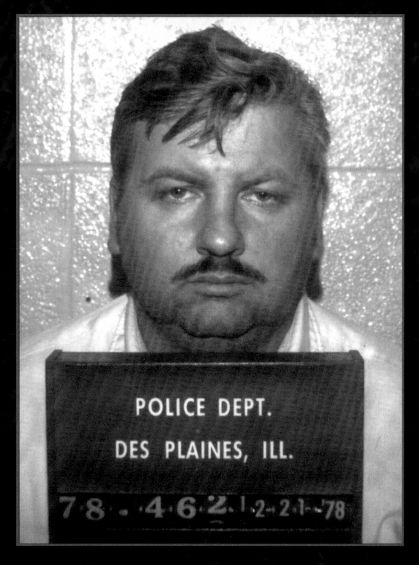

John Wayne Gacy, shown here in a mug shot from December 21, 1978, has had a tremendous impact on popular culture, influencing the archetype of the creepy or killer clown.

But all was not well with Gacy. He had an attraction to teen boys. In May 1968, twenty-six-year-old Gacy was sentenced to ten years for violently sexually assaulting a male teenage employee. His wife swiftly divorced him. Because of good behavior, Gacy was able to leave prison in just a year and a half. His mother helped him set up a new life in Chicago, where Gacy became a building contractor.

In 1972, he married Carole Hoff, a divorcee with two children. She moved in with Gacy, and they became hugely popular in the neighborhood, throwing parties and barbecues. Gacy volunteered often for the local Democratic Party. The same year he married, Gacy also killed his first victim. A fifteen-year-old boy named Jack McCoy was at the bus station in Chicago late at night. He had a bus to catch the next morning, but nowhere to go that night. Gacy drove by and told the boy he could stay at his house for the night. He stabbed McCoy to death and buried him in the crawl space of his house and covered the area with cement. Three years later, he killed again, and a stench began to devlop in the house. He told his neighbors and his wife that the smell came from a dead rat, and they somehow bought the excuse.

In 1975, Gacy was leaving homosexual pornography around the house and told his wife that he preferred men to women. After they divorced that year, the murders came in rapid succession from 1976 to 1978. He'd either pick up drifting boys at the bus station or lure respectable local teenage boys to his house with promises of work. He would often ask his victims if he could show them a trick with handcuffs. When he got the handcuffs on, he would restrain the boy to a chair or bed. He'd muffle his victims' screams by stuffing clothing in their mouths. Then he would force himself on them sexually. When he was done, he would strangle them. Sometimes

The gutted remains of John Wayne Gacy's home in Illinois were photographed in 1979, just before the structure was demolished. Investigators found the skeletons of twenty-nine bodies that Gacy had stowed in the crawl space and around the grounds of his property.

he would use a tourniquet to strangle them so he could watch them die slowly. Often, he killed two boys on a single night. Most were buried in the crawl space, but he also dumped five victims in the Des Plaines River when he ran out of space.

On December 11, 1978, he killed fifteen-year-old Robert Piest. He was a stock boy at a local pharmacy who went to Gacy's home to find out more about a work offer. When Piest was reported as missing, a friend told police that Piest had gone to Gacy's house. A search of Gacy's home soon revealed the full extent of his crimes. During his imprisonment, details emerged of Gacy's troubled childhood. His father was abusive and often beat him, and at age eleven, a swing hit Gacy in the head, which gave him regular blackouts. Gacy was found guilty of thirty-three murders and put to death by lethal injection on May 10, 1994.[1,2,3]

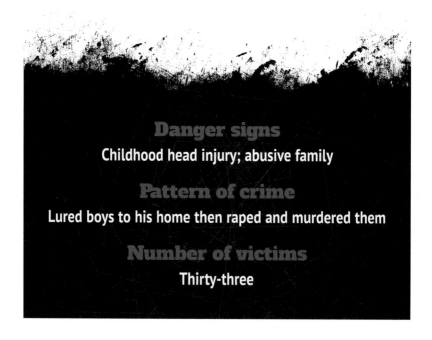

Danger signs

Childhood head injury; abusive family

Pattern of crime

Lured boys to his home then raped and murdered them

Number of victims

Thirty-three

Dennis Lynn Rader
aka "The BTK Killer"

Born: March 9, 1945

Profession: Electronics technician,
installed alarms

Motive: Lust

Date of capture: February 25, 2005

Date of death: Serving ten consecutive
life sentences

By all appearances, Dennis Rader was a pillar of his community in Park City, a suburb near Wichita, Kansas. He was married for thirty-three years to the same woman, and he was the father of a son and daughter. He was an active member of the Lutheran Church and had been elected the president of its church council. He was a Cub Scout leader. He earned an associate's degree in electronics and a bachelor's degree in administration of justice. He served in the US Air Force.

Rader was trained as an electronics technician, and from 1974 to 1988, he worked at the Wichita-based office of ADT Security Services. Part of his job was to install home security systems, which many people in his area wanted because a local serial killer had them living in fear. Little did his customers know that the killer was the very man installing their protection systems.

Modern-Day Serial Killers

Despite his very normal daily life, Rader had dark desires. His sexual desires were tied to killing, and he felt compelled to make that fantasy a reality. Rader admired other serial killers such as Jack the Ripper, Ted Bundy, and Son of Sam, and he saw himself as one of them. He claimed that he and his fellow serial killers all had a "Factor X" in common. This Factor X was a darkness or demon that controls his desire to kill, and he recognized he had it when he was a young teenager. As a child, he tortured animals (hanging a dog and cat). He also claimed to have been dropped on his head when he was young; many murderers have had some sort of brain trauma at a young age. He had an interest in sadomasochistic porn and bondage as a teen. At eighteen, he was peeping in the windows of neighbors and stealing panties. Later, when his fantasies turned to actual murder, Rader would keep panties from his victims and wear them himself out of a perverse pleasure.

Rader carefully stalked his victims like a predator, studying their daily habits and where they lived. On January 15, 1974, he killed his first victims. He had a fantasy about killing Julie Otero and her eleven-year-old daughter. He broke into their home on this day, and found that the husband, Joseph, and their nine-year-old son were also in the house. He held the family at gunpoint, tied them up, put bags over their heads, and then strangled all but the young daughter. He brought her to the basement and hanged her. He sexually pleasured himself at the sight.

Rader saw himself as one of the great serial killers, and he wanted to be recognized for his work. In October of 1974, he placed a letter in a book at the Wichita Public Library detailing the Otero family murders. In 1974, Rader stalked and killed a young woman, and then in 1977, Rader killed two more. In early 1978, Rader sent

Dennis Rader, known as the BTK Killer, was a seemingly average citizen, active in his community, and a devoted family man. He terrorized the Wichita, Kansas, area by breaking into homes and torturing and murdering the people inside. Rader was ultimately undone by clues obtained from packages he sent to the media.

a nursery-rhyme poem to the local newspaper referring to one of his murders. A month later, Rader sent another note to a local TV station. He had a desire for fame and claimed responsibility for the murders of the two women, and he suggested several names for himself, including the BTK ("bind, torture, kill") Killer.

Rader went on to kill three more women between 1985 and 1991. The police could not find the killer, and the trail went cold for years. In 2004, Rader resurfaced, sending media and authorities several letters, taunting them that the BTK Killer was still out there. In one of his contacts with police, he sent a floppy disk to them. By checking metadata in the documents, police were able to trace the disk back to Rader's church and ultimately to Rader himself. This was the break that police needed, and by February 25, 2005, they had enough evidence to arrest Rader. He confessed to his crimes, and on August 18, 2005, he received ten consecutive life sentences—one life sentence per murder victim.[4,5,6]

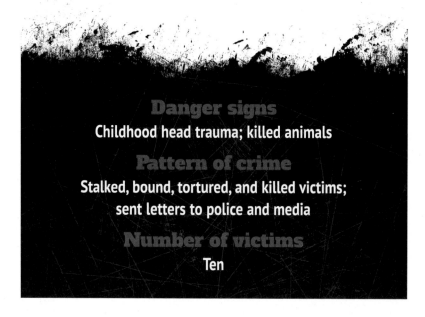

Danger signs

Childhood head trauma; killed animals

Pattern of crime

Stalked, bound, tortured, and killed victims; sent letters to police and media

Number of victims

Ten

Kenneth Bianchi and Angelo Buono

aka "The Hillside Strangler"

Born: May 22, 1951; October 5, 1934

Profession: Security guard; car upholsterer

Motive: Lust

Date of capture: January 13, 1979

Date of death: Serving a life sentence (Bianchi); September 21, 2002 (Buono, in jail)

In many ways, Kenneth Bianchi seemed like a normal person and an unlikely murderer. He was handsome, six feet (1.83 meters) tall, slim and muscular. He held a job and had a steady girlfriend. Along the way in his life, however, there were indicators that he was not the model person he appeared to be.

Adopted as a baby, Bianchi grew up in Rochester, New York. His mother remembered young Kenneth as a frequent liar and regular bed-wetter. He often fell into trance-like states. At age nine, his parents sent him for psychiatric evaluation for "involuntary urination, tics, absenteeism, and behavior problems." When he was thirteen, his father died, but Bianchi showed little emotion. Although he was an intelligent young man, he underperformed at school. At age twenty, he married a girl his age, but his wife left him after a few months. The experience may have left Bianchi bitter about women and relationships. He threw himself into community college, taking

Kenneth Bianchi testified during a pretrial hearing in Los Angeles Superior Court on July 6, 1981. Bianchi and his cousin Angelo Buono committed a string of murders that authorities for a time attributed to one person, dubbed "The Hillside Strangler" by the press.

and he dropped out. He took up work as a security guard and stole items on the job.

Looking for a change at age twenty-five, Bianchi made a decision that would alter his life. He moved to Los Angeles to live and connect with his cousin Angelo Buono, an auto upholsterer. Buono had a reputation for being abusive toward women, and yet he seemed to have no trouble getting into relationships. After being turned down for a job with a local police force, Bianchi obtained work as a security guard and bought phony psychology degrees. He rented office space as a psychologist, but saw little business.

Meanwhile, his sexually aggressive cousin showed him how they could use false police badges and convince prostitutes to have sex with them. They then decided to act as pimps and control prostitutes and the money they earned. A prostitute tricked Bianchi and Buono by giving them a false list of male customers. Enraged by the deception, the two men sought revenge. On October 17, 1977, they took out their anger on a nineteen-year-old prostitute named Yolanda Washington, strangling her and dumping her body in a cemetery.

The killing seemed to release a manic bloodlust in the two men. Over the next two months, the pair abducted, killed, and tortured two more prostitutes and five middle-class girls. One was fourteen, and another was just twelve years old. The women were strangled, but evidence showed that the killers were also experimenting, using lethal injection, electric shock, and carbon monoxide poisoning.

The city of Los Angeles and the police department were on edge. The LA Sheriff's Department dubbed the killer "the Hillside Strangler" because the murders all took place in the hills above Los Angeles. Some detectives said the murders were the work of more than one man because of how the bodies were moved.

During this period of murder, Bianchi lived an ordinary life. He had a girlfriend, Kelli Boyd, who was pregnant with their child. He even applied for a job with the Los Angeles Police Department. He was turned down, but he went for ride-alongs in police cars with authorities.

In February of 1978, around the time of the birth of Bianchi's son, Sean, the duo killed their final victim. Around this time, Bianchi

Along with Bianchi, Angelo Buono raped, tortured, and killed young women in the Los Angeles hills during a period from 1977 to 1978. Given up by his cousin in order to receive leniency, Buono was sentenced to life imprisonment. He died in 2002 at Calipatria State Prison in California.

told Buono of his ride-alongs with police, and this led to a huge argument between the two. To get away from the tension with Buono and the pressures of a new family, Bianchi decided to move to Bellingham, Washington. The strangling murders in Los Angeles stopped, and the trail to find the killer went cold.

Bianchi, however, could not seem to stop his dark urges. On January 12, 1979, he hired two local college girls to house-sit for him. He murdered them both. Bianchi was quickly identified as a suspect. Evidence clearly showed he was the killer, and during a search of his home, police found items that connected him to the Hillside stranglings. Ever the liar, Bianchi tried to fake multiple personality disorder to be declared insane and possibly escape the death penalty. He testified against Buono to receive leniency. He and Buono were both sentenced to life in prison. Buono died in 2002.[7,8,9]

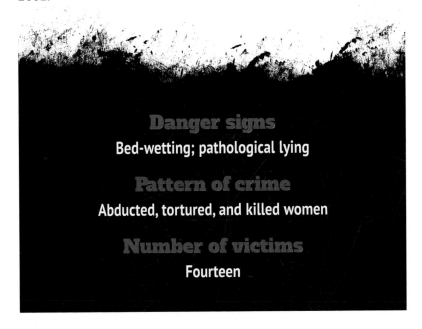

Danger signs
Bed-wetting; pathological lying

Pattern of crime
Abducted, tortured, and killed women

Number of victims
Fourteen

Chapter 4

THE CHARMERS

Not all sexual predators are unmemorable, average citizens or outwardly creepy individuals. Some are especially pleasant and agreeable and skilled at fooling people. Kenneth Bianchi overlaps into this category slightly, but serial killers Ted Bundy and Rodney Alcala are poster boys for charming serial killers. Both came across as very personable and attractive to women when they wanted to.

Ted Bundy

Born: November 24, 1946
Profession: Law student
Diagnosis: Psychopath
Date of capture: February 15, 1978
Date of death: January 24, 1989
(executed)

On the surface, Ted Bundy appeared to be bound for success. As a young man, he was a good student, had many friends, worked for the Republican Party, and even had his own political ambitions. By most accounts he was smart, charming, and normal; however, it turned out his good nature and average-American-boy persona was all an act.

Many serial murderers have traumatic childhoods, but Bundy has said that he had a wonderful upbringing. In interviews, he has said that he was never physically, emotionally, or sexually abused. His parents were dedicated and loving. He regularly went to church with them. As a child, Bundy was shy and often bullied. He did have a tendency to lie. Bundy believed that pornography played a role in his development. When he was twelve or thirteen, he found graphic pornography in the trash that depicted sexual violence, and he felt that contributed to shaping him into a rapist and killer. His sexual fantasies were of a violent nature. As he grew older, he felt he needed to make these fantasies a reality. Drinking alcohol also helped him reduce his inhibitions and pursue his brutal urges.

Handsome and charming, Ted Bundy had no trouble attracting women who would be his victims. This all-American young man was able to murder dozens of women across the country until the FBI finally tracked him down.

At age twenty-one, Bundy met Stephanie Brooks. She was slender with long brown hair parted in the middle—a trait most of his future victims would hold. He was totally in love with her, but after about a year she broke up with him because he seemed to lack ambition. Bundy was devastated. Gradually, he regained his spirit and poured himself into classwork and other activities. He worked with local Republican political campaigns in Seattle. He answered calls for a suicide hotline and apparently showed great empathy and support to callers. He also saved the life of a three-year-old from drowning and received a commendation from the Seattle police.

In 1973, he was accepted into law school and was dating a new woman, Meg Anders. That year he took a business trip for the Republican Party and secretly met up with Stephanie Brooks. He still had strong feelings for her. Brooks was impressed with his new spirit of determination. They even spoke of marriage. But by the beginning of 1974, something seemed to have snapped in Bundy. He broke off his relationship with Brooks, an act that crime analysts believe was his way of getting revenge on her for breaking up with him in the first place. He continued to see Meg Anders.

He also committed his first murder. He bludgeoned to death twenty-one-year-old student Lynda Ann Healy on February 1, 1974. Bundy killed five more women over the next few months. In July 1974, two women disappeared from a Washington State park. When police were called in to search, witnesses reported seeing a man with his arm in a cast going by the name of Ted. He was asking women if they could help secure a sailboat to his Volkswagen Beetle. In an anonymous call to the police, Meg Anders identified her boyfriend as a possible suspect. Police interviewed him, but found his demeanor to be so nice and harmless that they dropped him as a suspect.

Bundy moved to Utah in the fall of 1974 to go to law school. That October he abducted and killed three more women. *Time* magazine said that he sometimes displayed the lopped-off heads of victims in his apartment and slept with their corpses "until putrefaction made it unbearable." In the beginning of 1975, he traveled to Colorado and killed four women there. That year, he was pulled over by police in Salt Lake City. Upon searching his car, they found a crowbar, a face mask, rope, and handcuffs. Carol DaRonch was called in by police to identify Bundy. He had attempted to kidnap her in a Salt Lake City shopping mall, but she escaped. Bundy received a one-to-fifteen-year sentence for his attempted kidnapping.

As he was serving this sentence, police connected him with the murders of young women in Colorado. He was taken to Aspen to stand trial. While waiting trial, he escaped from prison and spent about eight days hiding out in Aspen until he was recaptured. He was put in a cell but again figured out a way to escape through the passageway in the ceiling. He dropped down into a janitor's closet and strolled out of the prison without any trouble. Two weeks after his escape, he had made his way to Tallahassee, Florida, where he murdered again.

On January 14, 1978, he broke into a sorority house at Florida State University and savagely attacked four women, killing two. Bite marks on one of the victims would be crucial in convicting Bundy. His final victim was twelve-year-old Kimberly Leach. In Pensacola, Florida, Bundy was driving a stolen vehicle. A suspicious policeman ran a check and discovered the car was stolen, so he pulled it over and discovered Bundy driving. Bundy fought the officer, but he was

Aspen, Colorado, police officers use scent dogs to search for Ted Bundy after his escape from the Aspen Courthouse. Bundy was on the run for six days before police were able to find him.

finally subdued and put under arrest. The evidence against Bundy was overwhelming, and on January 24, 1989, the forty-three-year-old was put to death in the electric chair.

Bundy had said that once he was satisfied and released his violent energy, he would return to being a normal person. "I led a normal life, except for this one, small but very potent and destructive segment that I kept very secret and close to myself," Bundy said in an interview with James Dobson the day before his death.[1,2,3,4]

Danger signs

Frequent liar; violent fantasies triggered
by pornography

Pattern of crime

Wore a cast to trick women into helping him,
then abducted, raped, and murdered them

Number of victims

Thirty or more

Rodney Alcala
aka "The Dating Game Killer"

Born: **August 23, 1943**

Profession: **Photographer**

Motive: **Lust**

Date of capture: **July 24, 1979**

Date of death: **Sentenced to death on March 30, 2010**

The Dating Game was a popular TV show in the 1960s and 1970s. On this show, three bachelors would compete to win the affection of a bachelorette by answering questions she posed. In 1978, Rodney Alcala appeared on the program as Bachelor Number 1. Host Jim Lange introduced him as "a successful photographer who got his start when his father found him in the darkroom at the age of thirteen, fully developed." Alcala was charming enough to beat out the other bachelor contestants and win a date with the bachelorette, Cheryl Bradshaw. After the show was over, however, Bradshaw refused to go out with him because she found him creepy.

If the TV show producers had only researched a little deeper, they would have known that Alcala had already been convicted of raping an eight-year-old girl in 1968. He was imprisoned for almost three years for that crime and released on parole for good behavior. Within two months, Alcala had broken his parole by giving marijuana to a

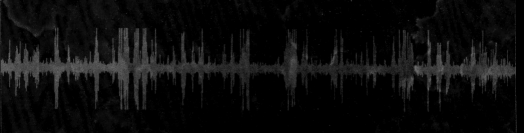

Rodney Alcala was convicted for seven murders, but he may have killed anywhere between 50 and 130 women. Alacala managed to elude authorities for years until he was sentenced to death for the murder of Robin Samsoe, a twelve-year-old girl.

thirteen-year-old girl, who said she had been kidnapped. Alcala went back into prison and served another two years.

What the show's producers would *not* know at this point is that Alcala was already a killer and had murdered several women. When he was eventually captured, prosecutors said that Alcala was cruel in the manner he toyed with women. He would often strangle them to a point of unconsciousness, let them revive, and strangle them again—repeating the process until he finally killed them.

Growing up in Los Angeles with his mother and sisters, Alcala's childhood might have been scarred by one incident. Psychologists have said that abandonment by his father may have left deep-seated emotional scars. At age twenty-one, he suffered a nervous breakdown while serving in the US Army. A military psychiatrist diagnosed him as having an antisocial personality disorder and had him discharged. This type of disorder is characterized by a blatant disregard for others, which manifests through violation of the rights of others.

After serving jail time for his rape of the eight-year-old girl, he raped and murdered two women. In 1978, around the time he appeared on *The Dating Game*, he landed a job as a typesetter at the *Los Angeles Times*. At the time, police were looking for the Hillside Strangler, and they interviewed Alcala as a possible suspect. Also that year, he sexually assaulted and strangled a young legal secretary using a shoelace. During this time, he was also taking many photos of young women and men, presenting himself as a professional fashion photographer. Most of his photos were explicit, and police suspect that some of the subjects in his photo collection may have met an untimely end.

On June 20, 1979, twelve-year-old Robin Samsoe, an aspiring gymnast from Huntington Beach, California, vanished while on

Alcala, who considered himself a playboy of sorts, appeared on the popular television show *The Dating Game* in 1978. On this show, contestants asked a series of three questions to three bachelors they could not see. At the end of the show, they were tasked with choosing one of the bachelors with whom to go on a date. Alcala was actually chosen, but upon seeing him, the contestant declined the date.

her way to a ballet lesson. A witness saw someone fitting Alcala's description with Samsoe. In investigating Alcala, police found earrings belonging to Samsoe in a locker that he rented. In 1980, he was sentenced to death for Samsoe's murder. In 2003, new DNA analysis revealed that Alcala was the killer of several other women. He posed the corpses in carefully composed positions, and analysts suspected that Alcala had a sexual gratification from dead bodies.

In defending himself, Alcala blamed the military for making him a killer, and he played "Alice's Restaurant" by Arlo Guthrie to the jury. The lyrics include "I mean, I wanna, I wanna kill. Kill. I wanna, I wanna see, I wanna see blood and gore and guts and veins in my teeth. Eat dead burnt bodies. I mean kill, Kill, KILL, KILL." In 2010, New York authorities found that Alcala was the likely murderer of women there in the 1970s. On March 9, 2010, Alcala was sentenced to death, and he is currently awaiting execution on death row.[5,6]

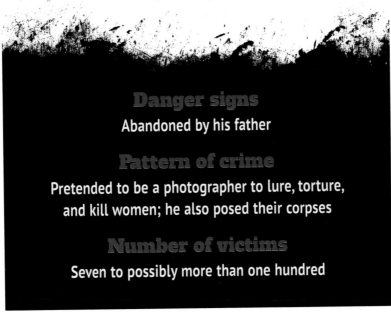

Danger signs
Abandoned by his father

Pattern of crime
Pretended to be a photographer to lure, torture, and kill women; he also posed their corpses

Number of victims
Seven to possibly more than one hundred

Chapter 5

NECROPHILIACS

Necrophiliacs (also called thanatophiliacs) derive pleasure from sexual contact with corpses. Their sexual fantasies revolve around a person being dead. Many serial killers may exhibit this perversion, but Dennis Nilsen and Edmund Kemper were especially driven to be with dead bodies.

Dennis Nilsen

aka "The Muswell Hill Murderer" and "The Kindly Killer"

Born: November 23, 1945
Profession: Police constable, job center civil servant
Motive: Lust
Date of capture: February 9, 1983
Date of death: Serving life in prison

Dennis Nilsen was considered a quiet, mild-mannered civil servant. He was a gay man who had trouble maintaining any serious relationship. He often felt very lonely. At the end of 1978, Nilsen began picking up gay men in bars in the London (England) neighborhood of Soho, which had a new and vibrant gay scene. Nilsen would bring men home and then strangle them as they slept. Nilsen killed for companionship: He would bathe and dress their corpses and keep them in his home for extended periods. Sometimes he would watch TV with the corpses and talk with them; other times, he would have sex involving the bodies. Nilsen described how with one victim he bathed his corpse in the tub and washed his hair. He described the body as being quite floppy. He dried off his new dead friend and tucked him into bed, secure in the thought that he would have company for a while. One victim was tattooed and had body ink that read "Cut here" with a dotted line around his neck. Nilsen though

Dennis Nilsen was found guilty of murdering six men and attempting to murder two others and was sentenced to life in prison in 1983. Nilsen was extremely lonely and kept company with his victims even after he had killed them.

it was a funny joke, but he was all too happy to oblige the tattoo's instructions.

After killing, Nilsen put his victims' bodies underneath his floorboards. When the victims began to rot, he made a bonfire in the backyard and burned their remains. To help dispose of the remains, he would cut the body into pieces and flush them down the toilet. He killed eleven men in such a fashion over the course of three years and was never pursued by the police during this time.

When he moved in 1981, he chose an apartment in an attic. He felt that living upstairs might help temper his killing, but it didn't. In fact, this would prove to be his undoing, and experts speculated that he wanted to get caught. After killing his fourteenth victim (the third in his new home), he was flushing body parts down the toilet when the pipes became clogged. A plumber called in to fix the problem discovered what looked to be human flesh and bits of bone. He contacted the police, who went to call on Nilsen. When they told him that they found human remains in the pipe, Nilsen expressed disbelief. A detective pushed ahead and asked Nilsen straight out, "Where is the rest of the body?" Nilsen calmly answered, "In two plastic bags in the wardrobe. I'll show you." They also found three heads in the cupboards.

On the way to the police station, Nilsen told them that he thought he had killed fifteen or sixteen people since 1978. The remains were uncovered, and several survivors also came forward to testify about Nilsen's murder attempts on them.

Nilsen had tried to help analysts figure out what made him into a murderer. His father was an abusive drunk and was not present in his life. His parents divorced when he was four, and he and his mother went to live with her parents. His grandfather died when

This is the kitchen of the London apartment where Nilsen dissected and disposed of his victims. The kitchen has been removed from the London flat and is now on display at the Scotland Yard Crime Museum.

Nilsen was six, and the unexpected sight of his dead grandfather may have traumatized him. For a long time, Nilsen had led a respectable life—he served in the British Army and became a corporal. He worked as a constable from 1972 to 1973 and enjoyed the camaraderie. He went on from there to work in a job center. In 1975, Nilsen moved in with a male flatmate, whom he liked, and although they weren't romantically involved, they seemed to develop a comfortable and quiet domestic life, taking care of a dog and cat, gardening, etc. When the roommate left in 1977, Nilsen's loneliness grew, and the murders began.

A jury found Dennis Nilsen guilty of six murders, and he was sentenced to life in prison on November 4, 1983.[1,2,3]

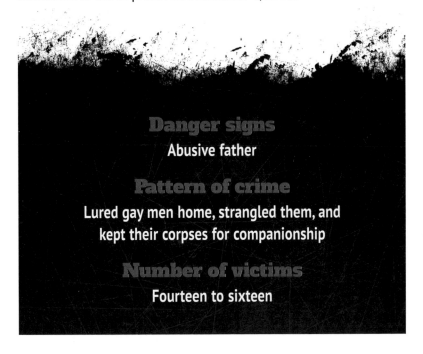

Danger signs

Abusive father

Pattern of crime

Lured gay men home, strangled them, and kept their corpses for companionship

Number of victims

Fourteen to sixteen

Edmund Kemper

aka "The Coed Killer"

Born: December 18, 1948

Profession: Laborer with the California Highway Department

Motive: Lust

Date of capture: April 24, 1973

Date of death: Serving a life sentence

The first thing that struck most people who met Ed Kemper was his size: He was (and still is) a giant. As a young man, he stood six foot nine inches (2.1 m) tall and weighed around 300 pounds (136 kg). His size alone made him a threatening presence. That combined with his perverse desire to kill and associate sex with murder made him especially dangerous. Kemper has traced back his mental disorder to a troubled childhood. He felt close to his father, but when he was nine, his parents divorced, and his mother packed up him and two sisters and moved to Montana.

He resented his mother for the breakup, and he felt unfairly treated by her. His mother was an alcoholic and often blamed him for all her troubles. She was critical of his hulking size and mocked him for being weird. She told him that no woman would ever love him. This attitude made him very insecure. The insecurity eventually

His mother made him live in the basement, partially out of a growing distrust and a fear that he might harm his sisters. He started to display some of the telltale signs of a developing killer. He enjoyed cutting off the heads of his sisters' dolls. He liked to play a game with his siblings called "gas chamber," where he pretended to be executed and mimicked convulsions. At age ten, he buried the family cat alive. Once it was dead, he decapitated it, put its head on the end of a stick, and displayed it in his bedroom as a trophy. When the family cat was replaced, he pinned it down and lopped off the top of its skull, showering himself in blood.

When one of his sisters teased him about having a crush on a teacher, she suggested he should kiss her. He answered, "If I did that, I'd have to kill her first." His budding sexual fantasies involved killing everyone in town and having sex with their corpses.

As he entered his early teen years, his mother sent him to live with his father. He hoped to reconnect, but his father found him difficult to deal with, and so at age fifteen, he was sent to live with his grandparents on a farm in California. He felt like he was being shipped off into isolation. He called his grandfather senile and his grandmother emasculating. He knew they kept a .45 automatic handgun in the house, but he had promised not to touch it. His grandparents were leaving on a shopping trip one day, and he noticed his grandmother had stuffed the gun in her purse. He felt this was a sign they did not trust him. Kemper became angry and shot his grandmother dead. When his grandfather walked in, Kemper killed him, too, because he knew he'd be mad at him for killing her. He later said he just wondered what it would feel like to shoot her.

Kemper was declared mentally ill, diagnosed with paranoid schizophrenia, and committed to a secure state mental hospital for

Edmund Kemper is taken to court in Pueblo, Colorado. Kemper murdered his grandparents, six hitchhikers, and his mother and her friend before calling the police to confess. Before he could even finish his call, police were at his home to arrest him.

the criminally insane. As a highly intelligent person, he impressed doctors, and in five years he was considered to be reformed. But the psychiatrists were wrong. He was released into the care of his mother, who was now living in the Santa Cruz area. Despite issues of past abuse and psychological problems related to his mother, the twenty-year-old moved back in with her. For a while, he led what seemed like a reformed life. He took community college classes. He took an interest in law enforcement and applied to be a state trooper but was rejected.

At age twenty-three, he was working for the California Highway Department. After being hit by a car while riding his motorcycle, Kemper received a $15,000 settlement. He used the money to buy a new car, which he customized so the driver's side door could not be opened from the inside. He also bought a gun, a knife, and handcuffs. Because of his injury, he was unable to work for a while, so he took up a hobby—picking up female hitchhikers. The first few he picked up, he let go.

On May 7, 1972, he followed his darkest desires. He picked up two eighteen-year-old female college students, drove them down a dirt road, and stabbed them to death. He put their bodies in the trunk and drove back to an apartment where he was now living. On the way back, he was almost caught when a police officer stopped him for having a broken taillight. He let Kemper off with just a warning. Kemper brought the bodies into his apartment, photographed them, dissected them, cut off their heads, and had a sexual experience. He put their remains in plastic bags and buried them in the mountains. He kept their heads a bit longer and then disposed of them in a ravine.

He killed again in a similar way four more times. The media referred to him as "The Coed Killer." The day after he killed one girl, he had scheduled visits with court psychiatrists to check on his mental health.

They declared him safe, and Kemper was relieved to have outsmarted them. He took the head of one woman he killed and buried it in his mother's garden, saying that his mother had always wanted someone to look up to her.

In his last act of complete madness, Kemper murdered his mother on Easter weekend in 1973. He killed her with a claw hammer while she slept. He decapitated her and engaged in sex with her corpse. He threw darts at her head and tried to put her vocal cords down the garbage disposal. He could not get rid of them down the sink, which he thought seemed appropriate—he couldn't eliminate the source of her complaining and screaming. He then invited a friend of his mother's over to the house and took her life as well. He drove away and at some point stopped the car, called the police, and surrendered. The court found him guilty of eight murders, and he was sentenced to life in prison, a term that he is still serving.[4,5]

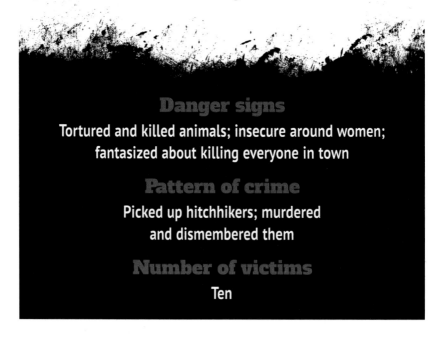

Danger signs

Tortured and killed animals; insecure around women;
fantasized about killing everyone in town

Pattern of crime

Picked up hitchhikers; murdered
and dismembered them

Number of victims

Ten

Chapter 6

ANGELS OF DEATH

The serial killers known as "Angels of Death" are health care professionals who get a great exhilaration from controlling the life and death of the patients in their care. They often thrive on the attention they receive for "caring" for the very ones they are killing.

Kristen Gilbert

Born: **November 13, 1967**

Profession: **Nurse**

Motive: **Thrill**

Date of capture: **November 24, 1998**

Date of death: **Serving four consecutive life terms plus twenty years**

Kristen Gilbert started her adult life with a promising future ahead of her. She did very well academically in high school and graduated one and half years early. By age twenty-one, she had earned her nursing degree and was married. Although she had many positive qualities, the mother of two sons had a real darkness inside of her. Even from a young age, she displayed behaviors that were troublesome.

Born Kristen Strickland, she was considered by some friends and family to be a pathological liar. She often threatened to commit suicide, but the threats never seemed serious. Ex-boyfriends said she was physically and verbally abusive. When she was twenty, while working as a home health aide, she scalded a mentally disabled child, leaving him with burns on 60 percent of his body. The incident was chalked up to an unfortunate mistake. Her marriage was tumultuous—during one argument, she chased her husband, Glenn Gilbert, around the house with a butcher knife.

This undated yearbook photo reveals the promise that Kristen Gilbert showed as a student. But with psychological problems and a career as a nurse, Gilbert soon began acting as an "Angel of Death."

In 1989, the twenty-two-year-old was hired at the Veterans Affairs Medical Center (VAMC) in Northampton, Massachusetts. After she began working in Ward C, hospital staff noted that an unusually high number of deaths were occurring. When many patients dropped dead in her care, some suspicions were raised. Most of her colleagues could not believe that she was the source of foul play. When any emergency came up, Gilbert always sprang into action and behaved as a professional nurse. She sent her coworkers flowers on special occasions. They saw her as a dedicated nurse and only teasingly called her "The Angel of Death."

Around the time the Gilberts' second son was born in 1993, their marriage was hitting the rocks. Kristen's friendship with a VA hospital security guard, James Perrault, was shifting to a more romantic nature. More patients began having emergencies and dying. Each time an emergency alarm rang in Ward C, however, Gilbert called Perrault to the scene so she could have time to flirt with him, even as patients fought for their lives.

Some nurses became concerned as more patients died. They voiced their suspicions, and a police investigation was launched. Investigators eventually found that Gilbert was stealing epinephrine, or adrenaline, and was injecting it in patients, inducing massive heart attacks.

The deaths seemed to correspond with her domestic troubles. When her marriage began to fall apart in the summer of 1995, she killed Stanley Jagodowski. In November 1995, Gilbert left her family and moved into her own apartment, showing her dedication to Perrault. Shortly after, she killed patient Henry Hudon. By February of 1996, she had killed two more. She reportedly murdered one patient under her care so she could leave early for a date.

Relatives of Gilbert's victims speak to the press outside federal court in Springfield, Massachusetts, on March 14, 2001. Gilbert was found guilty of first-degree murder in three deaths and guilty of second-degree murder in a fourth death.

When Gilbert found out she was under investigation, she phoned a bomb threat into the hospital. By spring, she had stopped working at the hospital. It took a while to build a case and gather evidence against Gilbert. Meanwhile, her relationship with Perrault unraveled in June of 1996, and she confided her murders to him. The next month, she took an overdose of medication and was admitted to a psychiatric ward. When she was released in October 1996, she was ordered by the court to live with her parents.

She was officially indicted for murder in November of 1998. In March of 2001, after a trial involving seventy witnesses and 200 pieces of evidence, Gilbert was found guilty of three counts of first-degree murder, one count of second-degree murder, and two counts of attempted murder. The fact is, Gilbert may very likely have caused many more deaths. She was on duty for half of the 350 deaths that occurred on her ward for the seven years she worked at the hospital from March 1989 through February 1996, according to the *Boston Globe*.[1,2]

Danger signs

Pathological liar; abusive to boyfriends

Pattern of crime

Injected adrenaline into patients
to induce heart attacks

Number of victims

At least four, but possibly many more

Richard Angelo

Born: April 29, 1962
Profession: Nurse
Motive: Emotional gain
Date of capture: November 15, 1987
Date of death: Serving a sentence of sixty-one years to life

Richard Angelo was a dedicated nurse working at a Long Island hospital. He was known as the go-to-guy in a crisis situation. At age twenty-five, he was entrusted with the care of the most critically ill patients. When he joined the staff of the Good Samaritan Hospital in Islip, New York, in April 1987, he worked the overnight shift, tending to heart attack victims and intensive care patients. In his leisure time, he volunteered as an emergency medical technician (EMT) with the Lindenhurst Volunteer Fire Department.

Hospital staff consistently praised Angelo's work, especially since he was dealing with so many emergencies. During September and October 1987 at Good Samaritan, thirty-seven patients experienced "code blue" emergencies while on his shift. Only twelve lived. On October 11, 1987, a crack appeared in Angelo's shining armor. After telling patient Gerolamo Kucich he would make him feel better, he proceeded to inject a muscle relaxant, pancuronium bromide, into his intravenous (IV) line. Patients can have a life-threatening reaction to this drug, and when Kucich received a dose, he

Richard Angelo is believed to have poisoned at least thirty-five patients at Long Island's Good Samaritan Hospital, where he worked as a nurse. Angelo claimed to be motivated by his need to be a hero.

immediately felt numb and unable to breathe. He was able to push a buzzer, summoning another nurse who saved his life.

The nurse was puzzled by the attack and ordered a urine test on the patient. The results found not only pancuronium bromide, but also another muscle relaxant called succinylcholine chloride. The patient was not supposed to be taking either of these. Police questioned Angelo the next day, and a search of Angelo's locker and home revealed vials of both drugs. Angelo was taken under arrest. Now Angelo's entire service had come into question. How many had he killed? An exhumation of several other bodies revealed the drugs in another ten people.

While attending a conference for EMTs on November 15, 1987, Angelo was arrested. Soon after, he confessed to giving unneeded muscle relaxants to an estimated two patients a week in September and October. He said he wanted to be the hero and rush on the scene to save the patients just in time. In a taped confession he said, "I wanted to create a situation where I would cause the patient to have some respiratory distress or some problem, and through my intervention or suggested intervention or whatever, come out looking like I knew what I was doing. I had no confidence in myself. I felt very inadequate."

Psychologists on his defense team said Angelo had dissociative identity disorder. This illness causes a person to disassociate completely from the crimes he or she commits. If Angelo had this disorder, he would be unable to realize the risk was causing to patients. The prosecution argued that he knew exactly what he was doing, and the jury found him guilty of two counts of second-degree murder, one count of second-degree manslaughter, one count of criminally negligent homicide, and six counts of assault. He is serving sixty-one years to life.[3,4]

Danger signs

Unknown

Pattern of crime

Caused patients to have respiratory distress
in order to heroically save them

Number of victims

Ten to twenty-five

Chapter 7

PROFIT OR GREED KILLERS

The serial killers classified as profit killers are motivated on some level to get more money, wealth, or possessions. They often get pleasure out of killing as well, but they have a strong drive for material gain. Note that one killer examined in this chapter, Adolfo Constanzo, would be categorized as a cult killer as well. He had a belief in black magic and a twisted or perverted view of religion. They may believe that killing is the only way to please the gods. They may have a grandiose view of who they are and what they can achieve. They may take advantage of others to do their bidding. They usually do not feel guilty for what they are doing because they feel like they are doing the right thing according to their distorted view of the world.

Dana Sue Gray
aka "The Shopaholic Murderer"

Born: **December 6, 1957**
Profession: **Nurse**
Motive: **Gain**
Date of capture: **March 16, 1994**
Date of death: **Serving a life sentence**

When Dana Sue Gray was asked why she bludgeoned, strangled, and stabbed old women, she said, "I had this overwhelming need to shop." Gray liked to have manicures and pedicures and dress fashionably. Appearances meant a lot to her. Authorities commented that she left murder scenes totally unruffled, hair in place, and barely a drop of blood on her.

Gray had an appetite for money and material possessions. Criminologists have said that she may have gotten her aggression and desire to buy things from her mother. A former beauty queen, her mother was described as a vain and forceful woman who frequently maxed out the family credit cards. Gray's father grew wary of her mother, who would get into volatile fights with those who angered her. When Gray was two, her father filed for divorce, and she rarely saw him after that.

At school, Gray did not get along well with others and she did not do well academically. At age fourteen, her mother was diagnosed with breast cancer. As she watched her mother being treated in the hospital, Gray vowed that she would become a nurse. When she graduated from high school, she pursued her nursing degree.

Described as blonde and beautiful, Gray participated in thrill sports and dated men who enjoyed these sports as well. She became an avid skydiver and dated her skydiving instructor. She mastered windsurfing and went out with a windsurfer. She also took up golf. She loved the active lifestyle and enjoyed trips to Hawaii where she pursued these activities.

At age thirty, Dana was ready to settle down. She married Bill Gray, a former high school classmate, and took his name. He loved sports as well and admired her beauty and fitness. They moved into a nice home in a gated community in Canyon Lake, not far from Los Angeles. But despite her good looks and their shared interest in athletics, the marriage hit rocky ground fast. Like her mother, Dana was not good with money and quickly plunged the couple deep into debt. She bought two cars, an ultralight airplane, and a couple of boats. She also spent a lot of money on alcohol.

Five years after their marriage, things were crumbling fast. She and her husband filed for bankruptcy to try to keep their Canyon Lake home. By June of 1993, they were divorcing, and Dana moved in with a new man. Her nursing work was not going well either. She was fired from her job at a hospital because she could not account for some missing opiate painkillers.

By February of 1994, Bill Gray was doing all he could to avoid Dana. He just wanted to move on with his life. Dana, however, wanted to meet with him. Although her motives were unclear, investigators have pointed out that Dana had a life insurance policy on Bill. They planned to meet on Valentine's Day, but Bill did not show up. Later that day, Dana went to visit a close family friend, Norma Davis, who was eighty-six and also lived in Canyon Lake. When Davis was found two days later, it appeared she had been strangled with a phone cord. She also had a knife sticking out of her chest and another knife sticking out of her neck. The old woman's credit cards were missing.

On February 28, 1994, Gray was driving through the Canyon Lake community with the five-year-old son of her boyfriend in the car. As she drove by, she spotted a neighbor, sixty-six-year-old June Roberts, raking leaves in her home by the golf course. She parked the Cadillac in front of Roberts's house and told the five-year-old to wait in the car. She asked Roberts if she could borrow a book. She later told different versions of why she attacked Roberts. In one version, Gray said she felt like Roberts and others in Canyon Lake were looking down on her for her failed marriage. Soon after they entered the home, Gray fiercely pounded Roberts's face with a wine bottle, grabbed a phone cord, and strangled her to death. She took her wallet and left.

Within an hour, she was putting Roberts's credit card to use, signing the woman's name as she purchased. First, she treated herself and the five-year-old to a meal at Bally's Wine Country Café. Then she stopped to splurge on an eyebrow wax and perm for herself and a fresh haircut for the child. She mentioned to the stylist that she was off on a shopping spree. Next up, she purchased a black suede jacket, a few pairs of cowboy boots, a pair of diamond earrings, two bottles of vodka, some treats for the dog, and a toy helicopter for the five-year-old. All went on Roberts's card.

A week and a half later, Gray had not been caught, and her desire to murder and shop came back. She went to an antiques

Dana Sue Gray would do anything to feed her materialistic lifestyle, including murder. Gray brutally killed three elderly ladies and attempted to kill a fourth, using their credit cards on subsequent shopping binges.

store and attempted to strangle Dorinda Hawkins to death. The fifty-seven-year-old shop worker, however, put up a fierce struggle and survived the attack. She was able to give police a description of her blond and athletic assailant. When police circulated a sketch of the suspect, Gray cut her hair and dyed it red. Even though she knew that police were now on the case, Gray would not stop. Within a week of attacking Hawkins, she drove to another community in Sun City. She stopped at the home of Dora Beebe, age eighty-seven, and asked if the woman could help her with directions. Beebe said she didn't have time, but she reluctantly invited Gray into her home while she went to get a map. Gray then strangled Beebe with a phone cord from behind. She brutally smashed her head in with an iron. Detectives later described the crime scene as one of the worst they had ever witnessed. Gray stole her credit cards and checkbook and again went shopping. She also used Beebe's checks, absent-mindedly writing "Dana Beebe" on one of them.

From witness descriptions, police identified Gray as a suspect, and she was soon arrested. When officers searched her home, they found new clothes with tags on them, new Nike Air athletic shoes, a purple boogie board, a $1,000 Trek mountain bike, and bottles of Opium perfume. On the day of her arrest, Gray was wearing the diamond earrings she had bought on Roberts's card. As they drove her to the police station, Gray enthusiastically told the police all about her new boogie board. In an interview, Dr. Patricia Kirby, a Baltimore psychologist and criminologist, said that Gray's motives appeared to go beyond greed and her dire financial situation—she seemed to take pleasure in the thrill of killing and celebrated each murder with a shopping spree. Gray was sentenced to life in prison without parole on October 16, 1998.[1,2]

Danger signs
Unknown

Pattern of crime
Murdered older women and stole their credit cards

Number of victims
Three

John George Haigh
aka "The Acid Bath Murderer"

Born: July 24, 1909
Profession: Car mechanic, ad copywriter, huckster
Motive: Gain
Date of capture: February 26, 1949
Date of death: August 10, 1949 (executed)

On the television show *Breaking Bad*, mild-mannered chemistry teacher-turned-meth cooker Walter White disposes of bodies using hydrofluoric acid. It is a body-disposal method you seldom hear about in real life. John George Haigh, however, was a real-life serial killer who got rid of his victims in just that way. On the surface, Haigh was charming. He was well-dressed, respectable, and well-mannered. His true personality, however, was one of a liar and swindler.

Haigh grew up in a religious family in Outwood near Wakefield in England. The Haighs belonged to the "Plymouth Bretheren," a congregation whose members believed they were not subject to the law of man but to "divine grace." From this background, Haigh may have gotten the notion that he was above the law and could do anything.

After leaving school, he landed a job as a car mechanic. He absolutely loved cars, but he detested dirt so much that he couldn't keep the job for long. He soon found employment as an advertising

John George Haigh, "The Acid Bath Murderer," was taken to court handcuffed to a policeman on April 1, 1949. Haigh was charged with murdering victims in order to collect money from their estates.

copywriter—inflating the truth was something that suited Haigh. As his career blossomed, he was able to afford a sporty Alfa Romeo car. When money from the company cash box went missing, he was fingered as the prime suspect and fired. On July 6, 1934, he married Beatrice Hammer, but the union was short-lived. Within four months of their wedding, Haigh was under arrest for a scam concerning certain fraudulent agreements, and his wife sought a divorce. He ran a successful dry cleaning business for a short time, but it didn't succeed.

He moved on to London, where he met the wealthy Donald McSwann, who employed him at his amusement arcade. Haigh toiled as his chauffeur and as an arcade game repairman. He met McSwann's parents, and they took an immediate shine to the dapper employee. But Haigh's taste for crime always drew him back in. He was arrested several times—for posing as a lawyer and for stealing goods. While in prison, he used his time to think of schemes that would make him rich fast, instead of working. He thought of targeting rich old ladies, and he wanted to be able to commit the perfect crime. Haigh studied legal books and took a special interest in the term *corpus delecti*, which means a crime must be proven to have happened before a person can be convicted of committing that crime. The term can also mean the physical evidence proving the crime was committed. This evidence may be a dead body. Haigh interpreted all this to mean "no body, no crime." He wanted to find the perfect way to dispose of bodies so he could commit the perfect crime. In a prison workshop, Haigh completely dissolved a rat in a container of acid. He had his answer for the perfect crime.

Out of prison in 1944, Haigh rented a workshop at 79 Gloucester Road in London. He placed a forty-gallon (151-liter) vat of sulfuric acid inside. Would it work? He decided to test it out. In 1944, he chanced upon his old boss, McSwann. Over drinks, McSwann told Haigh of his family's recent property investments. Haigh saw a route to riches. He set a plan in motion. He invited McSwann on September 9 to meet him at his workshop. He hit his old friend over the head with a blunt object, and with great effort, he dumped his body into the vat. He covered the barrel and went home to sleep as his former employer dissolved. The next day, all that was left of McSwann was sludge and a few clumps of bone and tissue.

Haigh poured the remains down the drain. He contacted McSwann's parents and convinced them that their son had gone off to Scotland to avoid being drafted. After some time, when McSwann still hadn't contacted them, his parents grew suspicious. Haigh launched the next stage of his plan. He convinced the parents to come to his warehouse on July 2, 1945, and they met the same fate as their son. Somehow, he was able to forge papers that allowed him to sell off the McSwann estate, giving Haigh a small fortune.

He lived off their wealth for three years, but his bad gambling habit drained his funds faster than expected, and he began to seek a new target. He befriended a new couple with discussions about music. In February of 1948, he shot them both dead and dissolved their bodies in vats of acid. Again, he forged papers that transferred their wealth to him.

He moved to Onslow Court, a place popular with wealthy widows. In February 1949, he befriended a widow there and convinced her to meet him at his workshop. She was soon in the acid vat like the others, and Haigh was the proud owner of her jewelry and fur coat. A friend of the widow grew suspicious of Haigh when the widow went missing. She knew that he was the last person she had seen.

Neighbors look on as officers search an abandoned factory in Crawley, England, in 1949. Investigators discovered the remains of Olive Durand-Deacon, Haigh's last victim. Haigh had shot the wealthy widow and then deposited her body in an acid bath to destroy the evidence.

She reported this to police, who soon discovered that Haigh had sold the widow's jewelry to a local shopkeeper.

On February 26, police arrested Haigh. While under arrest, he told a detective, "I've destroyed her with acid. You'll find the sludge that remains at Leopold Road. Every trace has gone. How can you prove murder if there's no body?" He went on to explain how he killed the others as well but that his guilt could never be proven without bodies. Detectives, however, did find the remains of his victims, including a foot and dentures. While on trial, Haigh claimed he was insane and had drunk the victims' blood. A court, however, found him guilty of murder. He was hanged on August 6, 1949.[3,4]

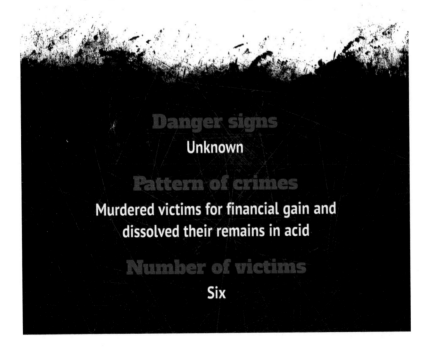

Danger signs

Unknown

Pattern of crimes

Murdered victims for financial gain and dissolved their remains in acid

Number of victims

Six

Adolfo de Jesus Constanzo

aka *"The Godfather of Matamoros"*

Born: November 1, 1962
Profession: Sorcerer, tarot card reader, model
Motive: Gain, religious rituals
Date of capture: Died before capture
Date of death: May 6, 1989

Adolfo de Jesus Constanzo grew up in Miami, Florida, and Puerto Rico. His mother was convinced that he had psychic powers and magical abilities. When he was just fourteen years old, she claimed that her son could predict future events with amazing accuracy. Months before President Ronald Reagan had survived an assassination attempt, Constanzo predicted that the president would be shot at and live.

Constanzo's father died when he was young, and so did his first stepfather. His second stepfather made money in the drug trade and the occult. Constanzo was attracted to dark magic. His mother and he were also arrested several times for shoplifting, theft, and vandalism. As a teen, he met a priest who practiced *palo mayombe*, which was known to be one of the world's most powerful and feared forms of black magic. Constanzo had a godfather who provided occult services and ceremonies to local drug dealers in Mexico, and this may

Known as "The Godfather of Matamoros," cult leader Adolfo de Jesus Constanzo engaged in ritualistic killings, of both strangers and of members of rival Mexican drug cartels.

have inspired Constanzo to follow a similar path. He made money reading tarot cards and picking up some modeling work.

In 1983, Constanzo fully devoted himself to *Kadiepembe*, who is the Devil in the palo mayombe religion. In 1984, he settled in Mexico City full time with a goal of establishing himself as a sorcerer and mayombe cult leader. He sold magical services to drug dealers, telling them that his rituals could protect them, and even make them bulletproof or invisible. Constanzo was charismatic and had an aura about him that convinced people he was connected to the spirit world, and many Mexicans believed in the powers of witchcraft. He held black magic ceremonies sacrificing animals, including goats, boa constrictors, lion cubs, and zebras. As his reputation grew, his clients included doctors, fashion models, nightclub performers, and even high-ranking law enforcement officials.

His wealth grew steadily as well, and he paid cash for a $60,000 condominium and $80,000 for a Mercedes Benz. Constanzo reached out to dangerous narcotics dealers and crime bosses because he knew they had money. He knew he had to impress them, so he pushed his rituals into darker territory. He ordered his disciples to dig up graves to get human body parts, which would be placed in a *nganga*, a cauldron for voodoo rituals.

At some point, Constanzo began kidnapping, torturing, and killing strangers. Although records show no complete tally of ritual-istic murders, twenty-three have been documented. As he provided his services to the Calzada crime family, Constanzo became convinced that he was the source of their success. In April 1987, he suggested that he become a full partner in their syndicate. When the family refused his request, Constanzo took action.

On April 30, Guillermo Calzada and six members of his household disappeared. About a week later, all seven were found murdered, their bodies dumped in the river. Their bodies showed signs of sadistic torture. Fingers, toes, ears, sex organs, and hearts were cut out. Two were missing their brains. Constanzo used the sacrifices to feed his cauldron of blood, claiming that it strengthened his powers and black magic. He began building his own illegal drug business.

As the cult grew in power, Sara Aldrete joined Constanzo's operation in 1987. Aldrete added a strange twist because she was a good-looking young college student attending school in Brownsville, Texas, who was pursuing a degree in physical education. When she met Constanzo, she fell under his spell, shed her old life, and became second in command. She was called "madrina"— the godmother or head witch. She supervised the followers as Constanzo took care of drug deals, and she initiated many sadistic tortures.

By 1988, Constanzo set up his base of operations on a ranch in Matamoros, Mexico, directly over the border from Brownsville, Texas. The ritualistic murders now escalated. After one man was dismembered, his body parts were dumped in the street, discovered by local children. Constanzo killed competing drug dealers and ordered his disciples to bring him innocent sacrifices. One disciple brought her fourteen-year-old cousin to be slaughtered. Sara Aldrete lured her old boyfriend to be killed.

Up until March of 1987, Mexicans were the victims, but in that month, Constanzo asked his disciples to bring him an American student. American students would come into Matamoros to drink. The disciples kidnapped twenty-one-year-old Mark Kilroy after a

Authorities uncovered multiple graves at Constanzo's Matamoros ranch. Twelve bodies were found at this site, including that of abducted US college student Mark Kilroy.

night of drinking. Kilroy was from the University of Texas, Austin. US law enforcers teamed with Mexican authorities and a massive search ensued. As their investigation spread, they came across a drug dealer at a checkpoint on April 1, 1989. After being arrested, the dealer, Serafin Hernandez Garcia, confessed to killing Kilroy. He also told them about Constanzo and his participation in fourteen ritualistic sacrifices. Garcia led officers to the ranch. Constanzo and cult members had fled, but the police found the remains of his victims, including the body of Kilroy, which had been mutilated and his brain removed. Over the next month, the discovery and arrests of cult members led police to find Constanzo. On May 6, 1989, police surrounded Constanzo in a house where he was living. He began shooting at police, but when he realized he could not escape, he ordered one of his followers to kill him.[5,6]

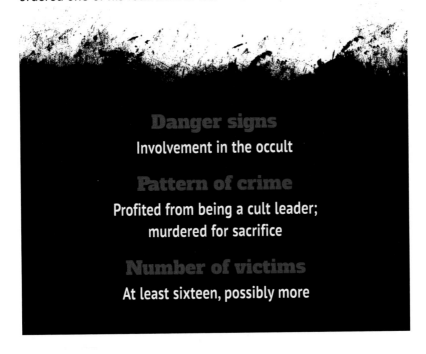

Danger signs

Involvement in the occult

Pattern of crime

Profited from being a cult leader;
murdered for sacrifice

Number of victims

At least sixteen, possibly more

Chapter 8

THRILL KILLERS

Some killers kill to right a past wrong. Others kill for gain, usually financial. Still others are sexually driven. But what about those serial killers who murder simply because they love to kill? Known as thrill killers, these people receive an almost addictive rush of adrenaline every time they kill, particularly from the planning that goes into it. They do not typically show any remorse about what they've done.

Elena Lobacheva
aka "The Bride of Chucky Killer"

Born: 1990, date unknown

Profession: Unknown

Motive: Thrill, mission to clean up Moscow

Date of capture: February 15, 2015

Date of death: Awaiting sentencing

Twenty-five-year-old Elena Lobacheva has a tattoo of her hero on her arm. *The Bride of Chucky* has been one of her biggest influences since the movie came out in 1998. Lobacheva has said that murderous doll inspired her to be a killer. Teaming up with her twenty-year-old friend Paul Voitov, the couple was responsible for gutting mostly homeless men and alcoholics in the streets of Moscow in Russia.

One middle-class bank employee also became their victim by mistake. The teller was merely meeting a friend in the park for a chat and a drink when the couple butchered him. Once arrested, Lobacheva told authorities that she and Voitov were on a crusade to clean up the city. They thought they were getting rid of human filth. They were trying to murder a specific group of people in an effort to eliminate them, so they could be categorized as missionary killers. The Russian media named the duo "The Cleaners."

Starting in July of 2014, they murdered men, stabbing them repeatedly, sometimes more than 100 times. They would then slice

Elena Lobacheva and Paul Voitov targeted homeless men on the streets of Moscow, Russia, in an effort, they said, to clean up the city. Known as "The Cleaners," the murderous pair stabbed vagrants and one professional they mistook for a homeless man.

open the bellies of the men and photograph their handiwork. Lobacheva said, "Randomly stabbing the body of a dying human brought me pleasure comparable to sexual pleasure." According to accounts from Russia, Lobacheva's home computer had step-by-step instructions on how to murder people. Police also found files with the victims' photos, including body parts cut off and stomachs cut open. Her apartment was described as being a complete mess, smelling of filth and her pet rabbit. Her mother has said that Lobacheva may be messy, but she's no killer. "She's supportive," said the mother. "She didn't kill. There is no anger in her eyes."

Lobacheva and Paul Voitov were caught on a security camera when they attacked a street cleaner. He fended them off with a screwdriver, and although the couple managed to stab him in the back, the cleaner made it to the police station, where he gave a full description of the pair. His testimony, plus footage caught on camera, led to their capture and incarceration. Their sentencing has yet to be determined.[1,2]

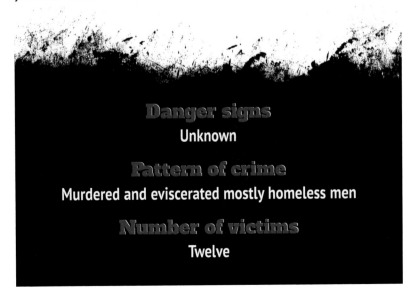

Danger signs
Unknown

Pattern of crime
Murdered and eviscerated mostly homeless men

Number of victims
Twelve

Lobacheva claims she was inspired to kill by the movie *The Bride of Chucky*, an installment of the popular *Child's Play* films, in which a doll is possessed by a serial killer.

Alexander Pichushkin
aka "The Chessboard Killer"

Born: April 9, 1974
Profession: Supermarket shelf stocker
Motive: Thrill
Date of capture: June 16, 2006
Date of death: Sentenced to life in prison
October 29, 2007

For Alexander Pichushkin, murder was an essential factor in living. He once said, "For me, life without murder is like life without food." He also said, "Human life is not too long. It is cheaper than a sausage." Pichushkin had an appetite for death, and he sated it in a local Moscow park in Russia. Often, he'd invite an elderly man to join him under the trees to enjoy a game of chess. After a friendly match he'd ask his new companion if he would like to take a shot of vodka by his dog's grave. They'd walk off to a secluded part of the park, and Pichushkin would bash in his or her brains with a hammer or pipe. " liked the sound of a skull splitting," he said. He typically threw the bodies of his victims in a sewer pit. Some were still alive when he dumped them in the sewer and they drowned.

Tracing the roots of Pichushkin's desire to take human lives is difficult. Little is known about his childhood. Pichushkin fell off a swing and hit his head when he was young. He began to act more hostile after the event, and his mother sent him to a school for children

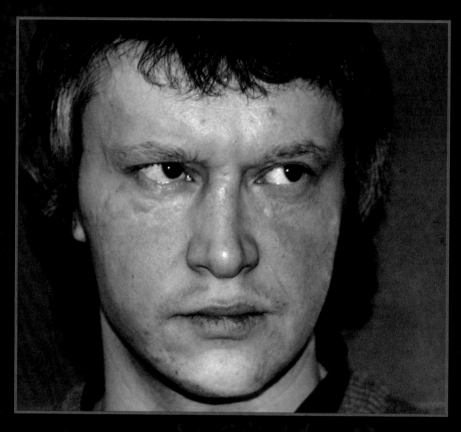

The Chessboard Killer, Alexander Pichushkin, strove to murder sixty-four people, one to represent each square on a chessboard. His modus operandi was to lure his victim with vodka, bludgeon him or her over the head with a hammer, and shove the bottle in the wound he'd created. Pichushkin says he killed so he could feel alive.

his cat died. He went to live with his grandfather, who was amazed at how good a chess player he was. He was bullied by other kids, and toward the end of his teen years, he suffered a huge emotional blow when his grandfather died. After this death, Pichushkin took to drinking heavily. He began threatening children in the park.

By age eighteen, he had urges to kill, and he acted on them. He had a crush on a girl named Olga, but she was in love with another boy. One day, he pushed the boy out of a window to his death. The police ruled it a suicide, but Pichushkin took credit for it years later, saying, "A first killing is like your first love, you never forget it."

Still, Pichushkin, an extreme loner, waited another nine years before beginning his killing spree in earnest, claiming many victims, including Olga. From 2001 until 2006, he murdered continuously. He branched out from elderly men and took the lives of younger men, children, and women. He said, "I felt like the father of these people, since it was I who opened the door for them to another world."

His last murder led to his arrest. In June 2006, he invited a woman with whom he worked to go for a walk with him in the park. She left a note for her son saying that she was going with Pichushkin. When police discovered the woman's body, they found a metro ticket in her pocket. They reviewed footage from the train station security cameras and saw Pichushkin walking with the woman.

While arresting Pichushkin, officers found a chessboard in his home. It had dates on more than sixty of its sixty-four squares—his goal was to fill the whole board. The dates referred to the murders he had committed, although authorities could only find that he killed forty-eight people. Police also uncovered a large stash of violent pornography in his possession, even though he did not sexually assault any of his victims. He was sentenced to life in prison on October 29, 2007.[3,4]

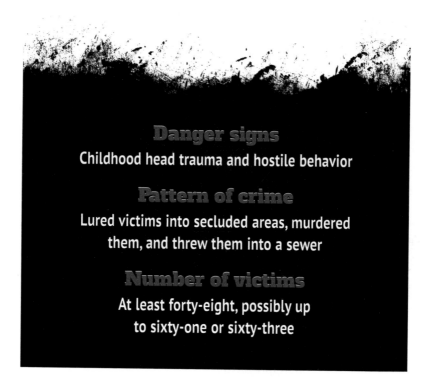

Danger signs

Childhood head trauma and hostile behavior

Pattern of crime

Lured victims into secluded areas, murdered them, and threw them into a sewer

Number of victims

At least forty-eight, possibly up to sixty-one or sixty-three

CONCLUSION

As the number of serial killings seems to have declined in recent decades, society may breathe a sigh of relief. Gruesome murders, including mass shootings, are continuing, however. Gaining a better understanding of the factors that shape a serial killer has given society a better chance of stopping a disturbed person before he or she can hurt others. Better security and improved police work have helped to nab suspects before they can wreak more havoc. Paying more attention to those who have mental health issues can surely help prevent heinous crimes and perhaps help people with severe mental issues lead productive lives instead of destructive ones. Understanding what causes people to kill can help stop murders in the future. Giving more care to young people who suffer trauma and increasing mental health care may help society keep serial killing at bay.

Psychopathy Quiz

Are You a Psychopath?

This quiz is designed to help give you some insight into people with psychopathic tendencies. While the quiz is not meant to diagnose psychopathy, it may also give you an idea about whether or not *you* have such tendencies.

Read each of the following statements and answer each honestly. Give yourself two points if the statement definitely describes you, one point if it somewhat describes you, and zero points if it doesn't describe you at all. Tally up the points to see where *you* sit on the psychopathy scale!

1. I'd rather be spontaneous than make plans.
2. I wouldn't have a problem cheating on a boyfriend or girlfriend if I knew I could get away with it.
3. I don't mind ditching plans to hang out with my friends if something better comes along—like a chance to go out with that hot new guy or girl.
4. Seeing animals injured or in pain doesn't bother me.
5. I love excitement and danger.
6. I think it's OK to manipulate others so that I can get ahead.
7. I'm a smooth talker: I can always get people to do what I want them to do.
8. I'm great at making quick decisions.
9. I don't get it when movies or TV shows make people cry.

10. Most people just bring problems upon themselves, so why should I help them?

11. I'm rarely to blame when things go wrong—it's others who are incompetent, not me.

12. I have more talent in the tip of my little finger than most people will ever have.

13. I am able to make other people believe my lies.

14. I don't feel guilty when I make people feel bad.

15. I often borrow things and then lose or forget to return them.

16. I skip school or work more than most people I know.

17. I tend to blurt out exactly what's on my mind.

18. I often get into trouble because I lie a lot.

19. I skip school and/or often don't get my assignments done on time.

20. I think that crying is a sign of weakness.

If you scored 30–40 points, you have many psychopathic tendencies.

If you scored 20–39 points, you have some psychopathic tendencies.

If you scored 0–19 points, you have no psychopathic tendencies.

Chapter Notes

Introduction

1. Christopher Beam, "Blood Loss: The Decline of the Serial Killer," Slate.com, January 5, 2011, http://www.slate.com/articles/news_and_politics/crime/2011/01/blood_loss.htm.
2. Victims of Violence, Updated February 16, 2011, http://www.victimsofviolence.on.ca/rev2/index.php?option=com_content&task=view&id=362&Itemid=52.
3. Katherine Ramsland, "Who Coined 'Serial Killer'?," *Psychology Today*, October 11, 2014, https://www.psychologytoday.com/blog/shadow-boxing/201410/who-coined-serial-killer.
4. Katherine Ramsland, "Triad of Evil? Do Three Simple Behaviors Predict the Murder-Prone Child?," *Psychology Today*, March 16, 2012, https://www.psychologytoday.com/blog/shadow-boxing/201203/triad-evil.
5. Jim Fallon, "Exploring the Mind of a Killer," TED Talk, July 2009, https://www.ted.com/talks/jim_fallon_exploring_the_mind_of_a_killer/transcript?language=en.
6. "The Psychology of a Serial Killer," Le Moyne College, http://web.lemoyne.edu/~Freemams/index_files/psych_serial.htm.
7. Meredith Galante, "There Are Two Types of Serial Killers and It's Easy to Tell Them Apart," *Business Insider*, April 12, 2012, http://www.businessinsider.com/types-of-serial-killers-2012-4.
8. "Types of Serial Killers," The Crime Museum, http://www.crimemuseum.org/crime-library/types-of-serial-killers.

Chapter 1: Psychotic Killers

1. "The Psychology of Serial Killers," DisturbingHorror.com, http://disturbinghorror.com/Serial-Killers/Serial-Killer-psychology.html.
2. "Richard Trenton Chase," Murderpedia, http://murderpedia.org/male.C/c/chase-richard.htm.

3. Rebecca Turner, "Psychological Analysis and History of Richard Trenton Chase," Academia.edu, June 2013, http://www.academia. edu/4302178/The_Psychopathology_of_Richard_Trenton_Chasse.

4. "Profile of Serial Killer Richard Chase," About.com, http://crime. about.com/od/serial/p/richard_chase.htm.

5. "Richard Muñoz Ramirez," Murderpedia, http://murderpedia.org/ male.R/r/ramirez-richard.htm.

6. "What Caused Richard Ramirez to Become the Night Stalker?," CNN.com, June 10, 2015, http://ireport.cnn.com/docs/DOC-1248463.

7. Richard Winton, "'Night Stalker' Richard Ramirez Died of Complications from Lymphoma," *Los Angeles Times,* June 17, 2013, http://articles.latimes.com/2013/jun/17/local/la-me-ln-nightstalker-died-of-complications-due-to-lymphoma-also-had-hep-c-20130617.

8. "Richard Ramirez," Bio, http://www.biography.com/people/ richard-ramirez-12385163.

9. "David Berkowitz," Bio, http://www.biography.com/people/david-berkowitz-9209372#arrest-and-imprisonment.

10. Tim Nash, "The Mind of Son of Sam," The Finer Times, http:// www.thefinertimes.com/Serial-Killers/the-mind-of-son-of-sam. html.

11. Nathan LaLiberte, "Son of Sam: David Berkowitz's History in Westchester County," *Westchester* magazine, May 2012, http:// www.westchestermagazine.com/Westchester-Magazine/May-2012/Son-of-Sam-David-Berkowitzs-History-in-Westchester-County/.

12. Dr. Nicola Davies, "Making of a Monster: David Berkowitz," Health Psychology Consultancy, July 30, 2012, https:// healthpsychologyconsultancy.wordpress.com/2012/07/30/ making-of-a-monster-david-berkowitz-son-of-sam/.

Chapter 2: Prostitute Serial Killers

1. "Gary Leon Ridgway," Murderpedia, http://murderpedia.org/male.R/r/ridgway-gary.htm.

2. "Gary Ridgway," Bio, http://www.biography.com/people/gary-ridgway-10073409.

3. "Murder Was the Case," Mass Appeal, April 29, 2015, http://massappeal.com/lonnie-franklin-jr-the-grim-sleeper-mass-appeal-issue-56/.

4. Christine Pelisek, "Inside Grim Sleeper's Home," *The Daily Beast,* December 19, 2010, http://www.thedailybeast.com/articles/2010/12/20/inside-lonnie-franklin-jrs-home-suspected-grim-sleeper-serial-killer.html.

5. Mandalit Del Barco, "Too Scared to Talk to Police, Stalker's Victims Open Up in 'Grim Sleeper,'" NPR, April 27, 2015, http://www.npr.org/2015/04/27/402050365/for-decades-a-serial-killer-stalked-black-women-in-la.

6. Chris Klint, "Serial Killer Robert Hansen Dies in Anchorage," TUU, August 21, 2014, http://www.ktuu.com/news/news/serial-killer-robert-hansen-dies-in-anchorage/27664412.

7. David Usborne, "Robert Hansen Dead: Alaska's 'Butcher Baker' Murderer Who Hunted His Female Victims Dies in Prison of Natural Causes," *Independent,* August 22, 2014, http://www.independent.co.uk/news/world/americas/robert-hansen-dead-alaska-s-butcher-baker-murderer-who-hunted-his-female-victims-dies-in-prison-of-9686672.html.

8. "Robert Christian Hansen," Murderpedia, http://murderpedia.org/male.H/h/hansen-robert.htm.

9. DeNeen Brown, "On Willy's Pig Farm, Sifting for Clues," *The Washington Post,* September 5, 2004, http://www.washingtonpost.com/archive/lifestyle/2004/09/05/on-willys-pig-farm-sifting-for-clues/81bb861b-7d29-4e4b-b717-0d2f02f2ddaa/.

10. "Pickton Described How He Killed Women, Former Friend Says," CBC News, July 16, 2007, http://www.cbc.ca/news/canada/pickton-described-how-he-killed-women-former-friend-says-1.635605.

11. "Robert William Pickton," Murderpedia, http://murderpedia.org/male.P/p/pickton-robert.htm.

12. Ken MacQueen, "How Serial Killer Robert Pickton Slipped Away," *Maclean's*, August 13, 2010, http://www.macleans.ca/news/canada/how-a-serial-killer-slipped-away/.

Chapter 3: Sexual Predators

1. Troy Taylor, "The Clown That Killed," Prairie Ghosts, http://www.prairieghosts.com/gacy.html.

2. John Kifner, "Gacy, Killer of 33, Is Put to Death as Appeals Fail," *The New York Times*, May 11, 1994, http://www.nytimes.com/1994/05/11/us/gacy-killer-of-33-is-put-to-death-as-appeals-fail.html.

3. "John Wayne Gacy," Bio, http://www.biography.com/people/john-wayne-gacy-10367544.

4. Tim Potter, "BTK Describes His Own Crimes," *The Wichita Eagle*, July 16, 2005, http://www.kansas.com/news/special-reports/btk/article1003753.html.

5. Josh Aden, "The Terrifying True Story of the BTK Killer," AllDay, http://allday.com/post/1070-the-terrifying-true-story-of-the-btk-killer/.

6. "Dennis Rader," Bio, http://www.biography.com/people/dennis-rader-241487.

7. "Defendant, in Unexpected Move, Tells of 'Hillside Strangler' Deaths," *The New York Times*, July 7, 1981, http://www.nytimes.com/1981/07/07/us/defendant-in-unexpected-move-tells-of-hillside-strangler-deaths.html.

8. "Kenneth Bianchi," Murderpedia, http://murderpedia.org/male.b/b/bianchi-kenneth.htm.

9. "Kenneth Bianchi: The Hillside Strangler," Crime + Investigation, http://www.crimeandinvestigation.co.uk/crime-files/kenneth-bianchi-hillside-strangler.

Chapter 4: The Charmers

1. Howard Chua-Eoan, "Ted Bundy, 1978," *Time*, March 1, 2007, http://content.time.com/time/specials/packages/article/0,28804,1937349_1937350_1937464,00.html.

2. James Dobson, "Fatal Addiction: Ted Bundy's Final Interview," Pure Intimacy, January 24, 1989, http://www.pureintimacy.org/f/fatal-addiction-ted-bundys-final-interview/.

3. Andrea Petrolini, "Antisocial Personality Disorder: The Case of Theodore Bundy," Infoboard: Abnormal Psychology, May 2002, http://www.psychohelp.at/h/college/abnormal/aspd.shtml.

4. "Ted Bundy," Bio, http://www.biography.com/people/ted-bundy-9231165.

5. Tracy Miller, "Serial Killer Rodney Alcala Won 'The Dating Game' Just Before Murder Spree," *The New York Daily News*, March 9, 2010, http://www.nydailynews.com/news/national/serial-killer-rodney-alcala-won-dating-game-murder-spree-article-1.174189.

6. Nicola Davies, "Making of a Monster," Health Psychology Consultancy, September 13, 2012, https://healthpsychologyconsultancy.wordpress.com/2012/09/13/856/.

Chapter 5: Necrophiliacs

1. Mark Duell, "Serial Killer Dennis Nilsen Brands Himself a 'Creative Psychopath' with an 'Overwhelming Desire to Kill' in Never-Before-Seen Letter," *Daily Mail*, September 23, 2014, http://www.dailymail.co.uk/news/article-2766495/Serial-killer-

Dennis-Nilsen-brands-creative-psychopath-overwhelming-desire-kill-letter.html.

2. "Dennis Nilsen: The Making of a Serial Killer," *The Scotsman*, November 23, 2009, http://beta.scotsman.com/lifestyle/dennis-nilsen-the-making-of-a-serial-killer-1-769305.
3. "Dennis Andrew Nilsen," Murderpedia, http://murderpedia.org/male.N/n/nilsen-dennis.htm.
4. "Edmund Kemper: The Co-ed Killer," Crime + Investigation, http://www.crimeandinvestigation.co.uk/crime-files/edmund-kemper.
5. "Edmund Emil Kemper III," Murderpedia, http://murderpedia.org/male.K/k/kemper-edmund.htm.

Chapter 6: Angels of Death

1. "Kristen Heather Gilbert," Medical Bag, April 26, 2013, https://www.themedicalbag.com/despicabledoctor/kristen-heather-gilbert.
2. Thomas Farragher, "Caregiver or Killer?," *The Boston Globe*, October 8, 2000, http://cache.boston.com/globe/metro/packages/nurse/part1.htm.
3. Eric Schmitt, "Nurse Known as Dedicated Worker," *The New York Times*, November 17, 1987, http://www.nytimes.com/1987/11/17/nyregion/nurse-known-as-dedicated-worker.html.
4. "Profile of Serial Killer Richard Angelo," About.com, http://crime.about.com/od/serial/a/richardangelo.htm.

Chapter 7: Profit or Greed Killers

1. Mara Bovsun, "Justice Story: Serial Killer Dana Sue Gray Offed Elderly Women So She Could Shop with Their Credit Cards," *The New York Daily News*, May 31, 2014, http://www.nydailynews.com/news/crime/justice-story-dana-sue-gray-article-1.1810400.

2. Kathy Braidhill, "To Die For," *Los Angeles Magazine*, December 1, 1998, http://www.lamag.com/longform/to-die-for/.
3. Charlotte Greig, *Evil Serial Killer: In the Minds of Monsters* (Dingley, Australia: Arcturus Publishing, 2010), p. 196.
4. "John Haigh: The Acid Bath Murderer," Crime + Investigation, http://www.crimeandinvestigation.co.uk/crime-files/john-haigh-the-acid-bath-murderer.
5. "Adolfo Constanzo," True Crime XL, August 4, 2012, http://truecrimecases.blogspot.com/2012/08/adolfo-constanzo.html.
6. "Adolfo Constanzo," Bio, http://www.biography.com/people/adolfo-constanzo-408870#cult-leader.

Chapter 8: Thrill Killers

1. Will Stewart, "Bride of Chucky Female Serial Killer Murdered Homeless People for Sexual Thrills," *Mirror*, February 27, 2015, http://www.mirror.co.uk/news/world-news/bride-chucky-female-serial-killer-5241191.
2. Will Stewart, "Russian Woman Accused of Stabbing 12 People to Death in Russia 'Admitted She Got Sexual Pleasure from Killing People and Kept Photographs of Her Victims with Their Stomachs Cut Open,'" *Daily Mail*, February 27, 2015, http://www.dailymail.co.uk/news/article-2971848/Russian-woman-accused-stabbing-12-people-death-Russia-admitted-got-sexual-pleasure-killing-people-kept-photographs-victims-stomachs-cut-open.html.
3. "Alexander Pichushkin: The Chessboard Killer," Crime Insider, August 16, 2015, https://crimeinsider.wordpress.com/2015/08/16/alexander-pichushkin-the-chessboard-killer/.
4. "Alexander Yuryevich Pichushkin," Murderpedia, http://murderpedia.org/male.P/p/pichushkin-alexander.htm.

Glossary

antisocial personality disorder—A chronic mental condition in which a person's ways of thinking, perceiving situations, and relating to others are dysfunctional and destructive, according to the Mayo Clinic. People with this condition typically have no regard for right and wrong and often disregard the rights, wishes, and feelings of others.

bipolar disorder—A mental disorder marked by alternating periods of elation and depression.

black magic—The use of magic and supernatural powers to achieve evil ends.

confiscated—Taken or seized with authority.

decapitate—To cut off the head.

disciple—A follower or student of a teacher, leader, or philosopher.

DNA—Deoxyribonucleic acid, the main constituent of chromosomes. The complete DNA of an individual is unique. DNA is present in all kinds of evidence, including blood, hair, skin, saliva, and semen. It is often left behind at a crime scene. Scientists can analyze the DNA in evidence samples to see if it matches a suspect's DNA.

emasculate—To deprive a man of his male role or identity.

gratification—Pleasure, especially when gained from the satisfaction of a desire.

inhibition—A conscious or unconscious restraint of a behavioral process, desire, or impulse.

ligature strangulation—Strangulation using some form of cord-like object—also known as garroting.

lithium—A drug used to treat mania that is part of bipolar disorder.

manipulation—Having control over others by having the ability to influence their behavior (emotions) and their actions so things can go in the manipulator's favor.

metadata—A set of data that describes and gives information about other data.

necrophilia—Sexual interest or physical sexual contact with dead bodies, irrespective of the sex.

occult—Supernatural, mystical, or magical beliefs, practices, or phenomena.

paranoid schizophrenia—A mental illness that involves false beliefs of being persecuted or plotted against.

perpetrator—Someone who has committed a crime.

psychopath—A person suffering from a chronic mental disorder with abnormal or violent social behavior.

sadist—A person who gains pleasure from inflicting physical or psychological pain on another.

Further Reading

Books

Houck, Max M., and Jay A. Siegel. *Fundamentals of Forensic Science*. San Diego, CA: Academic Press/Elsevier, 2015.

Lightning Guide editors. *Serial Killers: Jack the Ripper to the Zodiac Killer*. Berkeley, CA: Lightning Guides/Callisto Media, 2015.

Parker, R.J. *The Serial Killer Compendium*. Seattle: CreateSpace Independent Publishing, 2012.

Raine, Adrian. *The Anatomy of Violence: The Psychological Roots of Crime*. New York: Vintage, 2014.

Ronson, Jon. *The Psychopath Test: A Journey Through the Madness Industry*. New York: Penguin Publishing, 2012.

Slate, J.J. *Serial Killers (Encyclopedia of 100 Serial Killers)*. Toronto, Ontario, Canada: R.J. Parker Publishing, 2014.

Websites

Crime Museum: Crime Library
www.crimemuseum.org/crime-library

Murderpedia: The Encyclopedia of Murderers
murderpedia.org/

Videos

***Tales of the Grim Sleeper*. Directed by Nick Broomfield. 2014.**
Documentary that examines the notorious serial killer known as the Grim Sleeper.

Index